"Brutally honest, eminently practical, and wonderfully snarky, this book might save your teaching career, your joy in your vocational calling, and even your marriage. It is a true masterpiece of personal, pedagogical, and professional wisdom. I wish I'd had this volume before I completed my graduate degrees. I would have been much healthier, happier, and productive. Read this from cover to cover immediately, and then month-to-month starting before the-month-that-shall-not-be-named. Join the company of Eager Biebers!"

C. Ben Mitchell, Graves Professor of Moral Philosophy at Union University

"*The Flourishing Teacher* understands in wonderfully particular and empathetic detail the peculiar rhythms and challenges of the academic year. No matter where you are in your career, you will find winsome and practical advice for thriving in and, as importantly, out of the classroom. Through it all, Christina Bieber Lake is that trusted friend who has successfully navigated scholarship and teaching from whom we all wished we could get advice. Now we can."

Jennifer L. Holberg, professor of English at Calvin University, founding coeditor of the Duke University Press journal *Pedagogy*

"What a wonderful, invigorating, and encouraging book! I recommend it to anyone committed to the 'spiritual work' of college teaching. With honesty and confidence born of long experience, the author shares her vocational journey through the form of the academic year. Along the way, she offers splendid, practical wisdom while sustaining a graced tone of gratitude. *The Flourishing Teacher* is a vital addition to any professor's 'soul shelf,' but especially those of us who teach at church-related schools."

Paul J. Contino, Pepperdine University

"Christina Bieber Lake offers practical wisdom to educators in her new book *The Flourishing Teacher*. Drawing on her years of experience as both a K-12 teacher and a university professor, Lake guides educators through the landscapes of self-care, student engagement, and instructional strategies. This is a significant volume, bringing real-life tools to aid all who are involved in the teaching professions."

Ron Jacobson, dean of the School of Education at Whitworth University

"Dr. Bieber, as her students refer to her, has given those of us who teach a gift. With wit and transparency, this seasoned professor not only stimulates us to consider ways in which we can teach better but she provides us with specific strategies not only for the classroom but for maintaining sanity throughout the year—with specifics from managing emails to knowing how and when to say no to orchestrating the accomplishment of tasks on the to-do list. This book is not fluff; it is well researched, as Bieber Lake introduces us to resources that provide practical and soul-saving advice. Every teacher should read this book!"

Dennis Okholm, Azusa Pacific University

The Flourishing Teacher

Vocational Renewal for a Sacred Profession

CHRISTINA BIEBER LAKE

Academic

An imprint of InterVarsity Press
Downers Grove, Illinois

InterVarsity Press
P.O. Box 1400, Downers Grove, IL 60515-1426
ivpress.com
email@ivpress.com

InterVarsity Press® is the book-publishing division of InterVarsity Christian Fellowship/USA®, a movement of students and faculty active on campus at hundreds of universities, colleges, and schools of nursing in the United States of America, and a member movement of the International Fellowship of Evangelical Students. For information about local and regional activities, visit intervarsity.org.

Cover design: Autumn Short
Interior design: Jeanna Wiggins
Images: Wood rings composite © MirageC / Moment Collection / Getty Images
       Banana leaf textures © Neostock / iStock / Getty Images Plus
       Dark slate surface © Lilechka75 / iStock / Getty Images Plus
All interior figures © Christina Bieber Lake.

ISBN 978-0-8308-5284-0 (print)
ISBN 978-0-8308-5394-6 (digital)

Printed in the United States of America ♾

InterVarsity Press is committed to ecological stewardship and to the conservation of natural resources in all our operations. This book was printed using sustainably sourced paper.

Library of Congress Cataloging-in-Publication Data
A catalog record for this book is available from the Library of Congress.

P   25   24   23   22   21   20   19   18   17   16   15   14   13   12   11   10   9   8   7   6   5   4   3   2   1
Y   41   40   39   38   37   36   35   34   33   32   31   30   29   28   27   26   25   24   23   22   21   20

For Nicole

Thank you for being you

Contents

Acknowledgments

This book would not have come into existence if I had not formed "my own dang writing group." Thank you Nicole Mazzarella, Tiffany Kriner, and Beth Felker Jones for being my besties. You all make this job livable. Where would I be without your encouragement? I can't wait for bestie row.

I'm grateful for all the teachers who motivated or mentored me in the craft of teaching: NJ Scott, Victoria Kahn, Elizabeth Fox-Genovese, Gary Burge, and especially Jeffry Davis. Thank you for giving me such delicious ideas to steal and call my own. I also greatly appreciate David McNutt and the whole team at IVP Academic for embracing this project with enthusiasm.

Finally, thank you to Steve and Donovan for being the wonderful home I get to return to after the long day is done.

Introduction

A Long Obedience
in the Same Direction

Love from the center of who
you are; don't fake it.

ROMANS 12:9 *THE MESSAGE*

T his book was born out of the flu.

It was the day before classes began for my seventeenth year of teaching at Wheaton College and my twenty-first year of teaching overall. I had been severely ill for two days, leading me to reflect on the fact that I had never been so out of it at the start of the year. Beginning the academic year is always stressful, but my immune system had also been compromised by other stresses in my life at the time. So here I was in a situation that required the utmost energy with no energy to be had.

I badly needed inspiration. I needed to remember why I chose to do this crazy teaching thing. I needed to remember that I actually love my job and have always cared about more than a paycheck. And then it hit me. Toni Morrison wrote her first novel, *The Bluest Eye*, because it was a book she wanted to read. And I thought,

I need to write a book that I would want to read and reread for as many years as I retain this magnificent and incredibly difficult job.

Because it is magnificent. And incredibly difficult. It comes with highs and lows all tied to various seasons of the year. So it seemed logical to me to divide the book by what is most needed in each of those times. August, which I have dubbed "the-month-that-shall-not-be-named," has a very different set of challenges than does February, which I have often argued should be excised from the calendar altogether. (And if I were queen of the universe, I would, were it not for the fact that both my husband and a dear friend have birthdays in February.) This book follows the deep logic of the seasons: academic, but also environmental and liturgical, which of course are all related. When does the season of Easter make better sense than in the springtime? And when do teachers need a resurrection of their own if not in March and April? I hope the wisdom and universality of this approach motivates you to think through the seasons of your year and your life as an educator in a new way. That's my primary goal.

I'm a big believer in systems. Along the way in my career I've learned how to build systems that have helped me to flourish instead of just drag to the finish line. I've shared them with my colleagues for years, and I will share them with you here. I will also share the vast collection of little tricks I've learned to fool myself into joy. Because that is actually the way our brains work: researchers have shown that if you drink a wine you think is very expensive, you will enjoy it more. Similarly, when you take a placebo, your brain tells your body to get better, and it often actually does get better. Since the majority of what we do is by way of nonconscious cognition, it only makes sense to tap into that reservoir as deeply as possible. I hope this book provides many solutions as simple and revolutionary as putting your car keys in the same place when you get home and your lunch by the door after you pack it.

What I've learned about cognition and the stresses of everyday life is also what led me to design a book with more than one way to read it. We are all busier than we should be. To inspire you to change that is another one of my primary goals. In the meantime, you can read this book straight through, or you can pick it up during the month named. You can skip ahead to the chapters most relevant to you. Or you can choose from the list of things below and be directed to related chapters. Inspired by Gretchen Rubin's wonderful "Secrets of Adulthood" list, I offer "Things about the Scholarly Life I Learned the Hard Way":

1. Preparation expands to fill the time you give it (chapters one and two).

2. Keep the Sabbath and never work in the evenings (chapter nine).

3. Say *yes* in a timely way so that you can say *no* more often (chapter three).

4. Don't try to work when you are exhausted (chapters four and ten).

5. Form your own dang writing group (chapter eleven).

6. Receive grace, but achieve gratitude (chapters five and twelve).

7. Feed on student energy and protect your own (chapter two).

8. Reading is the most vital scholarly work we do (chapters six and ten).

9. Willpower is a limited resource (chapters seven and eight).

10. Classroom creativity pays back in energy what it costs in content (chapter nine).

11. Exercise always helps (chapter seven).

12. This *is* thriving (chapters five and twelve).

Finally, I hope this book inspires you to remember what you already know: a life spent teaching others is a truly fulfilling life. This *is* thriving. Friedrich Nietzsche is not one of the writers on my soul shelf, but he did write something that resonates with me: "The essential thing 'in heaven and earth' is . . . that there should be long obedience in the same direction; there thereby results, and has always resulted in the long run, something which has made life worth living."[1] Nietzsche may have meant this as a part of his critique of what he considered to be the slavish rules of Christianity, but he is on to something important here. Our lives our glaringly short and insignificant in the grand scheme of things. Even after we work very hard, the best we have to offer is a single lifetime's worth of the harvest produced in service of a worthy purpose. And this is exactly why we are the fortunate ones. The harvest we produce can be wheat and not chaff. We get to work out obedience not to a rarified idea but to the God of love. We get to inspire young people to grow intellectually and spiritually. We get to inspire them to live their lives with integrity, faithfulness, and joy, and to remind them that though they are seeds sown in weakness, they will one day be raised in power (1 Cor 15:43). We get to point them to the field that has the treasure in it.

Let's start teaching like we know it.

[1] Friedrich Nietzsche, *The Essential Nietzsche: Beyond Good and Evil and The Genealogy of Morals*, trans. Helen Zimmern (New York: Chartwell, 2017), 88.

August

Embrace the Lace

Around here the evil plant begins to show up in early July. I'll see it out of the corner of my eye when I'm enjoying a bike ride on the Illinois prairie path. It starts out small and green and innocent, but by the time it is fully grown, it mounts a silent, psychological attack so severe that only the toughest can survive.

Poison oak? No. Thistles? No, although thistles certainly have organized their own antigarden union in Illinois. Poison hemlock? Nope. It kind of looks like hemlock, but it doesn't attack the body. I'm talking about none other than *Daucus carota*, known here as prairie carrot. It seems harmless enough. In fact, it is a weed so beautiful that it takes its name from royal clothing: Queen Anne's lace. William Carlos Williams even wrote a poem about it, symbolizing also, of course, a woman:

> Here is no question of whiteness,
> white as can be, with a purple mole
> at the center of each flower.[1]

Lovely. So what's my problem with the delicate Queen Anne's lace? The problem is that when it first appears, it means that

---

[1]William Carlos Williams, *The Collected Poems of William Carlos Williams* (New York: New Directions, 1991), 1:162.

midsummer has passed. When it stands head-high with an explosion of white blooms surrounded by purple chicory flowers,

Daucus
carota

Queen Anne's
Lace

Figure 1.1. *Daucus carota*

it means that late summer has arrived. And late summer means one thing: the month-that-shall-not-be-named is here. It's August, and it's time to go back to class.

I love teaching. But it is also true that for most of us career teachers, when the month-that-shall-not-be-named arrives, it brings with it the sinking recognition that our lives are about to go from manageable to almost unmanageable practically over-night. We go from having time to work on that scholarly project every day to having time to work on it only once or twice a week—if we are lucky. We go from enjoying a lot of time with our families to disappearing into our offices or classrooms to grade an endless stream of papers. As a result, the month I have also called "one big, long Sunday night" rushes into our lives with a unique motivational challenge. How can we welcome the start of the year with as much energy as the students have when they return? What can be done about what I've come to call QALD, or Queen Anne's Lace Depression? Is there any way to remind ourselves that this vocation is a privilege? That we love this work? Is there any way to get inspired again?

The answer is simple, but it is not easy. We have to move toward the challenge, not run away from it. When we see the weeds, we have to decide to embrace the lace.

EMBRACE THE STUDENTS

The first thing to know about the month-that-shall-not-be-named is that you don't have to deal with it until it actually arrives. Unless you are in your first two or three years of teaching, if you are tinkering with classes in June or working on syllabi in July, you are just making it harder on yourself. After two years of fretting all summer long about my fall classes, I finally learned the first of my Things I Learned the Hard Way. Thing 1: class preparation expands to fill the time you give it. This truth is sometimes called Parkinson's law: any task will fill the amount of time you allot for it. Starting too soon was only hurting me and not necessarily improving my teaching.

Let me reiterate: this advice does not apply to first-year teachers, who have to invent everything afresh. One of the best choices I ever made was the summer I prepared my entire eighth-grade US history class in advance, right down to every overhead. But those of us who are experienced must learn to rely on that experience more than we feel like we should. I know that if I give myself a maximum of two weeks before the start of classes, I can complete the syllabi in time and feel more refreshed. This frees me to focus on the reason why I do this work: the students.

As is the case with any job, the daily, on-the-ground work can blind us educators to the larger perspective of what brought us here to begin with. Most of us went to graduate school because we had a deep passion for our discipline, a passion that typically translates into a desire to share that passion with other learners. We became teachers because we wanted to profess our love and persuade others to join us in it. Andrew Delbanco notes that "the true teacher must always be a professor in the root sense of the word—a person undaunted by the incremental fatigue of repetitive work, who remains ardent, even fanatic, in the service of his calling."[2] The question is, how do we get that passion back, year after year, semester after semester? Part of the answer to this question will be the subject of my next chapter, where I suggest ways to feed off of student energy. But in the middle of the month-that-shall-not-be-named, we are not with them yet. So what can we do?

My first piece of advice is to recognize that returning to that level of focus and intensity in the service of others is spiritual work, and it is very difficult. Since I discovered that I need to carve out time for this kind of work, I always plan a pre-school retreat. A couple of weeks before the start of every semester that I teach, I book a local hotel for two nights and use the time alone to pray for the ability to burst into my classes with joy instead of to limp into them with despondency. The somewhat bizarre and little-understood truth of most college professors and many high school teachers is that we are introverts. We are the ones who always loved to sit in a room with only our books for hours on end. We are the ones who got up early in the morning to do homework by ourselves. And like many other introverts, I married an extrovert (God bless him). I have only one child, and he is also an extrovert (God bless him). What this means is that when the semester gets really busy and I feel like I'm talking all the time, I begin to crave things that I know I don't actually want, like living by myself in a hut in the Outer Hebrides. A hotel may not have the sea spray and rugged landscape of Scotland, but if you want to, you can enjoy forty-eight hours without talking to a single person. When I go, that is my first goal, because I am preparing for a spiritual marathon.

I prefer to book a local hotel. Other educators I know drive farther away, relishing the time in the car and a more beautiful

---

[2]Andrew Delbanco, *College: What It Was, Is, and Should Be* (Princeton: Princeton University Press, 2014), 66.

destination. It doesn't matter, as long as you have large chunks of time to yourself without your spouse or children. Don't bring your computer. Just bring your journal, relaxing music, books from your soul shelf (see chapter 6), an iPad with Netflix—whatever it takes for you to relax and reenergize. The word *recreation* has lost its original meaning in our culture. We need time away from what we do in order to "re-create" ourselves into the best version of who we are. When I go, I bring a wonderful focusing tool that Jenn Giles Kemper designed a few years ago called *Sacred Ordinary Days: A Liturgical Day Planner*.[3] They have a version that starts with the calendar year, and one that starts with the school year, on August first. It is important to me to have real books and other tactile planning materials, and this one is beautiful and thought-fully arranged around the liturgical calendar. It begins with en-couragement to set a rule of life, then gives pages for reflecting and resetting goals. The daily pages include the daily office and space to write down priorities. Perfect for this pre-school retreat and for focusing all year long.

Beyond that, I bring only one school-related thing: my roster of students for the upcoming semester. It always helps me to re-discover the passion I have for teaching when I pray for my students by name. I do this precisely because I'm no saint. Since I have QALD and would rather stay at home and work on my latest book than go back to the classroom, I often have to write prayers in my journal for an embarrassingly long time just to remember that my vocation is to love and serve the students.

What has helped me most to re-create my passion for teaching is to pray for my students according to Ephesians 3. In this chapter, Paul tells his readers that it was by the grace of God he was made

---

[3]Available at www.sacredordinarydays.com.

a minister of the gospel, and that his one purpose is to share that hope with them. It is "for this reason," he continues,

> I bow my knees before the Father, from whom every family in heaven and on earth takes its name. I pray that, according to the riches of his glory, he may grant that you may be strengthened in your inner being with power through his Spirit, and that Christ may dwell in your hearts through faith, as you are being rooted and grounded in love. I pray that you may have the power to comprehend, with all the saints, what is the breadth and length and height and depth, and to know the love of Christ that surpasses knowledge, so that you may be filled with all the fullness of God. (Eph 3:14-19)

Praying along with Paul for our students is a powerfully focusing exercise. Note that Paul reminds us that every family in heaven and earth has a name because of God's love. Paul learned this from Jesus, of course. We are all God's creatures, with all of the hairs on our head numbered. Like the sparrows, none of us falls to the ground without our Father knowing it. These passages remind me that the purpose behind all of my work is to help others to learn how to be filled with all the fullness of God. I want my students to be rooted and grounded in love that has this much height, depth, breadth, length. I want them to know the love of Christ that surpasses knowledge. The fact is that all teachers need regular reminders that the important things lie somewhere beyond knowledge and in the realm of loving action. Although we are not primarily ministers of the gospel in our classes, we must never lose sight of the fact that it is souls that we are caring for when we teach. When classes start, I am able to share this prayer with my students and to say, truthfully, that I have already been praying for each of them. I have been praying that our class will be spiritually as well as intellectually transformative. And I hope and pray that by the end of our class they will agree with me that the two are inexorably connected. The time away helps me to recover that connection for myself.

EMBRACE WIN-WIN THINKING

Loving the students well is a question of focus. Most beginning professors and secondary education teachers are far too worried about their own performance and far too little focused on meeting the students where they are at. It is useful to remember that students often enter our classes completely terrified of us. They also never seem to know (for better or worse) that we are also terrified. So if we aren't careful, our first few weeks will devolve quickly into a bizarre comedy of mutual terrors. The good news is that is doesn't have to be that way at all. The month-that-shall-not-be-named is the time to reboot your classes, to think about why you do what you do, and to make this semester truly different. All of us would do well to remember that teaching is not about imparting knowledge to underlings. It is about inspiring fellow learners to want to think deeply about a subject that you know can transform them. If it cannot, then why are you teaching it? It is time to get a different career. Since you know that your subject can be transformative, you need to set up your classes accordingly. You need to embrace win-win thinking.

The first way that win-win thinking helped me as a writing and literature teacher was in forcing me to think about how my assignments match up with how students actually learn. There is, of course, no end of pedagogical literature out there about flipped classrooms and other strategies. I have learned a lot over the years from publications such as *The Teaching Professor* and the books I mention below. But here I want to simplify the issue by asking one question: in your classes, who does more work—you or your students? If the answer is you, then you are teaching in a lose-lose model. In my experience, here are examples of the three most common lose-lose models for educators.

1. You spend the first day of class reading your syllabus aloud then making the students go around the room and introduce themselves to the class. You lose because you have increased their terror, and they think that you think that they can't read. They lose because they are terrified. Terrified students do not participate in class discussions or deliver their best work.

2. You prepare complicated lectures for hours on end, and then deliver them in front of a snoozing or texting class. You lose time and energy, and they lose because you are doing all of the thinking for them.

3. You give them a big research essay assignment due at the end of the semester. You lose hours of your life writing comments on these papers that most of the students will never read. They lose because they don't read the comments.

I think you get the idea here. The goal is to transform all lose-lose approaches into win-win approaches before the semester starts. Let me take each of these blunders in turn and explain how I have tried to transform my own approach over the years. The point is not for you to do what I do but to think in a win-win way, whatever that means for your class and your teaching style. The win-win model is simple: you win when it means less mind-numbing work for you; they win when it means more meaningful and productive work for them.

Let's rethink the all-important first day of class. Whether you are an elementary school teacher or a college professor, the last thing that you want to do is to put terrified students on the spot. My favorite pop culture reference for this moment is the scene in the fantastic Disney movie *Inside Out*. The movie goes inside the head of its protagonist, an eleven-year-old girl named Riley, and turns each of her emotions into a character — Fear, Disgust, Anger, Sadness. The lead emotion is Joy (endearingly voiced by Amy Poehler), who struggles to stay in charge of Riley's "headquarters." When Riley's father is relocated to San Francisco, the drama begins. On the first day of school, an unsuspecting but well-meaning teacher asks Riley to stand up and tell the class about herself. Inside of Riley's head, Fear, who had been nervously going over possible horrible first-day scenarios, freaks out and shouts, "Are you kidding me? Right out of the gate! This is not happening!"

We all need to remember that most of our students feel this way in front of their peers and their teachers. While some of the students in class will know each other, many will not, even in a smaller college. My first goal is to help them want to be in my class with each other and with me. So although I hand out my syllabus on the first day, I never read it to them or go over assignments. Instead I tell them that we are going to spend the entire class period socializing. Why? Because students work better and learn more in a positive, energetic, and safe learning community. My second year of teaching I learned a marvelous way to help achieve this goal from an expert teacher and colleague, Gary Burge. He asks students to mix together in groups of three or four, learn one another's names, and answer an easy question like, "What is the most interesting movie you saw or book you read this summer?" He does several mixers like this the first couple of weeks of class. I modified this method to suit my purposes. On the first day, I have them mix and remix, and then I also encourage individual students to share (voluntarily) something about their new friends with the larger group. And every step of the way, I encourage them, listen to them, and explain exactly why we are doing this. After twenty years of teaching, I can't imagine how many times I've repeated this phrase, or one like it: "Research clearly indicates that we learn more if we become a trusting community. The more you are engaged, the more you learn." I tell them that I teach by discussion, and that it only works if we can be comfortable enough to take risks.

By the end of about forty-five minutes of these easy mixers, the students are feeling much more comfortable. We are laughing with each other, and they are seeing me as a human being who cares about them. Because I do. For the final mixer of the day I distribute a photocopy of a short passage from Parker Palmer's book *To Know as We Are Known*.[4] The passage addresses the importance of community in learning any subject. I ask them to read it aloud and discuss it with their group, and then we get back to the larger class and come up with a list of things that they are willing to do to help achieve this kind of class. I also ask them what they need from me. There are rarely surprise outcomes here. Students are smart and know a lot about being students. Completely unprovoked, they will name things like "do the reading," "listen to each other," "challenge myself not to be afraid," and so on. From this exercise not only do the students come up with their own ideas about how to contribute to a great class, they also learn my (loosely Socratic) *modus operandi* for every single class session: to get the students to come up with what I want them to learn. At the end of the first day I tell them we will go over the assignments slowly over the next couple of weeks, and then I dismiss them. When I taught night classes, I would wait until the second half of the class to talk about assignments, and even then I make sure not to spend too much time on them. Finally, I do these mixers at the beginning of class for as long as I think is necessary. Win-win.

---

[4]Parker J. Palmer, *To Know as We Are Known: Education as a Spiritual Journey*, repr. ed. (San Francisco: HarperOne, 1993), xvi-xvii.

Now that we've thought about what can be accomplished on the first day, let's move to the second lose-lose blunder, the stand-up-in-front-of-class-and-lecture model. You probably already have the idea that I never lecture for very long. But let there be no confusion: I make this choice not because I have no content to teach them or because I want to let them run wild with their own personal reactions to texts. We've all had teachers like this, and it is usually the result of laziness. I do have very specific content goals for each of my classes, but I try not to let those goals prevent me from reaching my primary goal: to get them to interact with the literature I am teaching in such a way that they want to talk about it that night in the dorm. If I have accomplished that, the class was successful.

A good way to think about this win-win approach comes from one of my teaching gurus mentioned above, Parker Palmer. In his marvelous book *The Courage to Teach*, Palmer explains that it is a false dichotomy to pit a teacher-centered class against a student-centered class. Neither of these approaches is desirable. The first places the teacher as an expert who filters the knowledge through to the students, who remain passive. The second tends to make the class into a free-for-all therapy session. The goal, argues Palmer, is a subject-centered class, where the teacher is a fellow learner who helps students discover what kinds of questions to ask and how to ask them. We form a community of truth whose goal is to be in relationship with the truth and with each other.

> As we try to understand the subject in the community of truth, we enter into complex patterns of communication — sharing observations and interpretations, correcting and complementing each other, torn by conflict in this moment and joined by consensus in the next. The community of truth, far from being linear and static and hierarchical, is circular, interactive, and dynamic.[5]

---

[5] Parker J. Palmer, *The Courage to Teach: Exploring the Inner Landscape of a Teacher's Life*, 10th anniv. ed. (San Francisco: Jossey-Bass, 2007), 103.

Palmer describes this community of truth idea at length in chapter four, which is well worth the price of the book. Wouldn't you rather have a dynamic class than a static one? One in which it was clear to the students that you were still learning alongside them? If you want to have a subject-centered class, it really helps to explain to the students *why* you want it to be this way. The further I get in my career, the more I recognize that intentionality is the key. Help them to get on board with your method. Put Palmer's chart on the board and discuss it with them. My rendering of the energy of these connections can be seen in figure 1.2.

Make your classroom conducive to learning: move the chairs in a circle. Use lectures only to lay a foundation for discussion. If you

Figure 1.2. Learning circle

prefer, use clickers to get them involved.[6] Assign group presentations—the ultimate win-win for a professor who gets exhausted by standing up front class after class. In addition to learning their topic (we all know the best way to learn is to teach), the students learn how hard your job really is. The point is that there are lots of different ways to achieve a subject-centered classroom. It is your orientation, not your method, that is the issue here. As James Lang puts it, "You can't fire the synapses in your students' brains. For the connections to be meaningful and effective, the students have to form them. Your task is to create an environment that facilitates the formation of those connections rather than simply lecturing at them about connections."[7]

Of course, I would love to do nothing more than have rich discussions with students about literature or philosophy or biology, but we know that we have to teach them how to write too. Recent research indicates that the amount of reading and writing required of students at the college level is dropping steadily year after year.[8] But writing about a text or a topic is still clearly one of the best ways to learn how to think, so we have to find a way to assign meaningful writing projects. Unfortunately, our thinking about teaching often tends to stop with our own undergraduate experience and training, so the third lose-lose blunder is still stunningly common among college professors. We need to ask, How effective is the research essay assignment the way that I have it set up right now? As with approaches to class time, there are lots of

---

[6]Clickers are handheld electronic devices whereby an instructor can conduct live, in-class polling of student opinions. You can use them to generate discussion or even to perform a kind of pre-test. In a science class you might ask, "What do you think is at the Earth's core?" The answers can be very revealing.

[7]James M. Lang, *Small Teaching: Everyday Lessons from the Science of Learning* (San Francisco: Jossey-Bass, 2016), 98.

[8]See Richard Arum and Josipa Roksa, *Academically Adrift: Limited Learning on College Campuses* (Chicago: University of Chicago Press, 2011).

resources available to help you to think through things like the portfolio system, how to use your school's writing center, and so on. I don't want to reiterate that research here. I only want to encourage you, again, to ask the win-win question: Do you spend more time assessing their work in your office or classroom than they actually do writing it? Science educators have their own version of this question: Are you actually doing your students' lab work while you are supposedly just trying to help? This is a bit of a hyperbole—but only a bit. Teachers need to remember that we were the ace students in our day, which is why we became teachers. We figured it out. But it is time for them to do the work, not us!

Again, my advice is to be intentional about sharing with your students why you do what you do. For if we assign written work without much by way of instruction and leave them twisting in the wind, we shouldn't be surprised by the result. They are programmed to try to learn what you want and produce that, but if they don't know what you want, how can they produce it? It is of course good to explain what you want, but it was transformative for my own teaching when I recognized that they need to know *why* I want what I want.

Thinking about "the why" has led to two big changes in my literature classes. The first is that I abandoned the research essay format for my 300-level American literature classes in favor of a short paper I call the brief interpretive response, or BIR. I was able to do this when I discovered that our majors had other, smaller classes better suited to requiring the research essay, and when I recognized that many of our students needed to go back to the first moves of literary analysis and build longer arguments from there. I learned the virtues of the short paper from my colleague and close friend, Jeffry Davis. Again, I adopted the assignment to suit my own purposes. When it is their turn, the students must write no more than 650 words about a text assigned for that day.

One of the novels I assign routinely in my American literature class is Jack Kerouac's *On the Road*. The pre-assigned students (usually three, worked out at the beginning of the term) must come up with an analytical and interpretive argument, write no more than 650 words, and then bring copies of their paper to class. When the day arrives, we spend part of the class period broken up into three groups in which the author reads his or her paper to the smaller group and gets feedback. The student has an audience besides me for his or her work, and the other students see how it can be done. Win-win.

The second thing I've changed is that I have increased the time I spend talking about how we learn to write. I give in-class writing assignments and explain that research indicates that forced, spontaneous writing is the best way to improve as a writer. I go over model student writing in class, helping them to make discoveries about what works and why and to think about an audience other than the professor. From those in-class discussions, students quickly learn that they need to let others help them to identify growth areas. They learn that often the most progress they can make on writing, aside from practicing it, comes from short meetings with me in my office. In ten minutes, I can usually identify with the student the one or two biggest areas they need to address before they turn their work in. Also, I always ask students to try to identify the issues before I do, because it is helpful for them and instructive for me. I don't read these drafts unless they can muster the motivation to come to my office and ask for help. Make no mistake: these short conferences are hard work and often brutal. When I'm forced to say something like, "You don't really have an argument here," tears flow. This is exhausting for everyone involved—hence my desire to move to the shack in the Outer Hebrides.

But here, as with everything, choose your pain. When I get the final copy of the BIR, which is due a week after the draft was due in class, I'm seeing something that the student has worked on for more than one night. I'm usually able to praise substantial progress. When I return the paper, I often get the chance to look the student in the eye and say, "You did it! Can you feel the difference between this paper and the earlier version?" For a student, this is the equivalent of finding the sweet spot on the bat and sending the ball over the fence. Why should we cheer any less for academic performance than we do for athletic performance? Students mostly want to be seen. They want to believe that you believe that they can do it. Win-win.

Again, the point is not to get you to try out my methods. Nor am I saying that my approaches satisfy all students—nothing does, and nothing ever will. The key to staying inspired to teach is to mesh your own gifts as a teacher with their deepest needs without killing yourself—or them. You must make uniquely personal discoveries about how to do this, and it takes time and experience. For example, I discovered from the feedback on my course evaluations that many students find me intimidating. Really? Lil' ol' me? To combat this, I commit a ton of extra office hours during the first two weeks of class and ask every student who has not had me as a teacher before to come in for a ten-minute chat. They get into my office, which for many of them is scarier than skydiving. I listen to them. I laugh with them, occasionally cry with them, and always learn amazing things. I learn about the student from Korea who transferred because he was tired of the party school atmosphere at the state school he attended. (Wheaton is routinely ranked in the top three of "stone cold sober" schools.) I learn about the one who is interested in a career in fashion—and I tell her not to look forward to my class attire, which is destined to disappoint. I learn about the one whose family farms flaxseed in North Dakota, and who is planning to return, Wendell Berry–style, after graduation. The world, sitting across from me! Lately I've started taking notes after their names in a beautiful hardback journal because it helps me remember them when I hear about things they've done later in their lives. There are all kinds of benefits to these meetings. They give me a chance to answer specific questions. They give me a chance to tell them I'm bad with faces and names and ask for patience if I blunder. Ultimately they see me as a human being, which makes them less afraid to be human themselves in front of me. Win-win.

Embracing the students and embracing win-win thinking is essential if you want to be able to enjoy this amazing calling to the full. Embrace the lace. But this is not enough. You also need to learn how to build systems to protect energy. Because when it comes to the marathon that is the academic year, there is no question that our energy is our most precious resource. To keep from burning out, we must think hard about our own work habits, where and when we do work, and how to have a quality home life. Maximizing energy is what September—and my next chapter—is all about.

FOR ADDITIONAL ENCOURAGEMENT

Bain, Ken. *What the Best College Teachers Do*. Cambridge, MA: Harvard University Press, 2004.

August is the time to read this book, as it will help you to rethink why you do what you do in your classroom. I find this kind of book truly inspiring.

Epstein, Mikhail, and Igor Klyukanov. *The Transformative Humanities: A Manifesto*. New York: Bloomsbury, 2012.

This book is excellent reading for humanities educators who need to get re-inspired about the potential of the humanities to make a difference in the world. When was the last time you thought about neologisms and the creative work that they do?

Palmer, Parker J. *The Courage to Teach: Exploring the Inner Landscape of a Teacher's Life*. 10th anniv. ed. San Francisco: Jossey-Bass, 2007.

I've been challenged by all of Palmer's books, but if I had to choose one for all professors to read, this would be it. Palmer understands how to tap into how students actually learn. He also stresses that we all teach our personalities, so we need to find a way to capitalize on that. This book has inspired thousands of educators at all levels to understand what it is we are doing when we teach. It is filled with paradigm-shifting practical advice about how to approach our craft with joy and passion. It emphasizes the love part of the "labor of love," which is what we all need.

Rubin, Gretchen. *The Happiness Project: Or, Why I Spent a Year Trying to Sing in the Morning, Clean My Closets, Fight Right, Read Aristotle, and Generally Have More Fun*. Rev. ed. New York: Harper, 2015.

Rubin is a kindred spirit, and this book has definitely impacted my life for the better, including giving me the idea of starting my own writing group (Thing 5). I can't get enough of creative problem solvers like her.

September

Eager Biebers:
Tap into Student Energy

One semester a few years ago I was having a particularly difficult time getting psyched up for classes. The delicious break had come to an end and I was still exhausted. I count on my breaks to return to feeling like a human being, but that had not happened. Now what?

I told my husband about how I was feeling, which turned out to be a great idea. Steve is an Anglican priest, and he is a wonderful encouragement to me. An extreme extrovert, he is so connected with everyone he knows in any way possible that at times I've been known to call him "Father Facebook." When he saw that I was struggling, Father Facebook proceeded to put out an appeal on social media: "My wife is having a hard time getting motivated to start the semester. All you former students, can you tell her why you were an Eager Bieber?" (My students call me Dr. Bieber.)

The comments started pouring in, and it was deeply encouraging. What I learned from this exercise is that my husband is amazing. I hate it for you if you are not married to someone like him. But I also learned the value of tapping into student energy. Students do this intense thing called college for only four years.

These years are, for the majority of students, jam-packed with intellectual and spiritual growth, new relationships, and the euphoric stress of cognitive stimulation. But we do this job year after year, and after a time it just gets, well, a little less exciting. When August and September come around, I try to remember what it felt like to be a college student. Not just the comedy of terrors I discussed in the last chapter, but the excitement of being in college classes at a thrilling time in your life.

Try it. Send yourself back in time to your sophomore or junior year, or whatever year it was for you when your brain turned on. It all felt deeply connected—not just the disciplines with each other but all of it with your own life. Though it was more than thirty years ago for me, if I think about it, I can get back to excitement, if only a little bit. What got me going when I was twenty was reading *Paradise Lost*, William Wordsworth, *Walden*, and Toni Morrison for the first time. I particularly remember spending hours reading *The Fairie Queene* one night during my sophomore year. I needed to declare a major, which felt to me like a kind of death of all my other interests. I was looking out of my gabled dorm window into the rain, thinking with great excitement about this text—how it brings together history, art, and philosophy all wound together in a deep symbolism. Boom—I had my major! And my career, as it turns out. Thinking about that day reminds me about all the different classes that got me to that point and beyond. The classes I loved the most were the ones that set the table and invited me to a multi-course intellectual feast. Those are the ones I try to emulate now.

When was the last time you thought about your burgeoning passion for your own discipline? Who were the teachers that developed that passion in you, and what exactly is it that drew you to them? The great news is that you are probably already that teacher for a student who is in one of your classes right now. You will never know about all of them, but you have to believe in your own eager Biebers, because they are the ones that make this all worthwhile.

There are several other practical ways to tap into student excitement and energy. The first is to spend time thinking about where most students are coming from and why they chose to go to college to begin with. Sure, many of them are concerned about finding jobs or getting into college, but the majority are much more idealistic about what these years are going to mean for them. I have an annual event in my own academic life when I devote myself to thinking about this: convocation. Since I'm one of those professors who revels in all the pomp of academia, I love convocation. All the students and faculty are gathered in mid-August in Edman Chapel for the first chapel of the year, which takes place before most classes convene. Faculty are on stage, colorful, stately, and far too warm in our hard-earned regalia. The president speaks. You can practically feel the anxiety of the first-year students and the joyful pride of the veteran ones. But the two moments I love most are the ones that also humble me every time.

The first is when one of the student leaders asks the faculty to stand, and he or she prays for us. This prayer is usually heartfelt and real. It is powerful to remember that the students are pulling for us. They want and need for us to succeed, for they are at college primarily for what they can learn from us. But my favorite moment is when the provost asks all the students to stand so that she can lead us in prayer for them. When they all stand up at once, it thunders in that room. You can hear and feel it. In the thunder of all of those young people standing up together, I get goosebumps. This is what it is all for! I literally shut my eyes and try to soak in their energy. This is not as "woo woo" as it sounds. When you are about to start a marathon, the glimmer of the finish line is what you want to keep in front of you. This is the moment when I reflect on the fact that any glory I have is from serving this group. I have four years to make an impact, and then that chance is gone.

Since the students bring the energy, a simple way to draw from it is to spend time with students outside class. At Wheaton we have a program called Passage that takes place just before the fall semester at HoneyRock, a beautiful property in northern Wisconsin. It is extra duty for faculty to serve in this program, but the ones who do are rewarded with the chance to feed off of the excitement of new students. When I asked faculty what they get from serving at Passage, all of them mentioned that it reminded them why they loved their jobs. Does your school have something like this? When I taught eighth and tenth grade, the school where I taught had a week-long wilderness trip in North Carolina for eighth graders, a kind of rite of passage. While I thought I was insane to sign up as a faculty advisor, I did it anyway. This trip transformed my relationship with the students and was deeply meaningful for me as well.

Often things that require a lot of energy give that energy back several fold. But even if you don't have the chance to do something like this, just keep your eyes open when the school year begins. Think about practices, even very simple ones like cracking jokes, that make the students feel like whole human beings, not brains on a stick. Tell them that you are happy to meet with them for lunch or coffee. If you are a high school teacher, go to your students' sporting events. Remember, students mostly want to be seen, and they want you to see them when they are at their best. After you show that you are interested in them, the motivated ones will seek you out, and it is inspiring to watch their wheels spinning.

Student energy is a vast, undertapped resource. Why do we keep doing boring things in our classrooms when our students are eager to join something exciting with us? If you have never invited the Holy Spirit to come into your classroom, please try it this year. This can be a very simple prayer: "Jesus, you promised us your Holy Spirit. Please be present in this class from this day forward. Give us your energy. We want to learn what you want to teach us." If you are in a public school, you will have to keep that prayer to yourself. But if you are in a private school, share your desire for God to be the one who keeps us interested in growing, even when the growing gets hard. Teaching is about creating an invigorating intellectual and spiritual experience for the students, and you never know when they are going to recognize it themselves. I like the way that the veteran educator Andrew Delbanco puts it:

> Every true teacher, after all, understands that, along with teacher and students, a mysterious third force is present in every classroom. Sometimes this force works in favor of learning; sometimes it works against it. This is because ideas must cross an invisible interval between the mind of the teacher and that of the student, and there is no telling when a provoking thought will succeed in crossing that space, or what exactly will happen to it during its transit from speaker to hearer. One never knows how the teacher's voice will be received by the student, in whose mind it mixes with already-resident ideas that have accumulated from prior experience and, perhaps, from other teachers. Sometimes the spoken word is nothing but noise that evaporates in the air or has no effect in the mind of the student beyond annoyance or confusion. Sometimes it can have surprising and powerful effects — yet it is impossible to say why or when this will happen for some students and not for others. The Puritan word for this invisible and inaudible force was grace.[1]

---

[1]Andrew Delbanco, *College: What It Was, Is, and Should Be* (Princeton: Princeton University Press, 2014), 48.

If you have invited the Holy Spirit into your classes, you cannot predict when your words will hit that sweet spot that begins a transformation. You cannot force or predict grace. But you've got to trust that God is working. Have you ever had what you thought was a very dismal day up front, only to find out later that a student had some deep need met, question answered, or thought stimulated by that very session? That is what we need to remember. It is not all about us. Thank God.

Finally, when it comes to drawing from student energy, it is great to keep an encouragement file. If you teach long enough, you will receive numerous notes from students, many of them pouring out their souls to thank you for mentoring them. They will even share some specific moments from years ago that you had forgotten. When you feel like you can't possibly go back for another year of teaching, pull these notes out. I keep some of mine in books in my home study and in my college office so that when I randomly stumble over the note, it speaks to my soul on the spot. A colleague recently posted an image of her file titled, "Why I Do This." You can keep an email folder for this purpose too. But whatever you do, don't read student evaluations if you are trying to get yourself pumped up for the semester. I'll discuss how to handle student evaluations in chapter ten, but now is not the time for them.

STUDY YOUR OWN ENERGY

As you remember how exciting it was to be an undergraduate or a student in her favorite high school class, this is also a good time to remember that there are substantial differences between the student years and your life as a faculty member. This should go without saying, but many faculty seem to forget that yes, you can live on pizza-fueled all-nighters like a student if you want to be really productive, but you can't maintain it. Students surge with adrenaline and can pack a lot into a late night, but they are twenty, and this is only four years of their life. Not to mention that they often burn out. Our careers are long (we hope), and burnout has much more serious ramifications.

So my advice for you for September is to think very hard about energy—not energy in general, but your energy. Where it comes from. When it's high. When it's low. What you have energy for, and what you don't. Some people are born with boundless energy. I am not one of those people, and it really annoyed me to discover this. After college I went to Louisiana to teach high school. It nearly destroyed me. I was twenty-two and yet could only crawl, utterly spent, toward the weekend. Every Friday night I became a zombie in front of the television in my tiny apartment, watching *X-Files* (with no lights on) and wishing I were Dana Scully. I dreaded every Monday. I was aware that other young people were going out with friends while I was by myself, making a deep furrow in my futon sofa. This condition did not reflect my desire: I wanted to have energy. I felt passionate about what I was doing, but I often didn't want to get out of bed. I was cursed, I felt, to be both a perfectionist and a low-energy person. I was very unhappy during those years.

There were several things I had to learn. First, for me, low energy is one of the primary ways that depression manifests itself. I didn't figure this out until after I had my first child, and I really wish I had figured it out earlier. I also didn't know that high school teaching was not the right work for a seriously studious introvert like me, and I was setting myself up for exhaustion and failure. I loved the books I was teaching, but the students didn't. I didn't respect the students because they didn't like the books. They didn't respect me because I didn't respect them, and the downward spiral began. I wilted. But from my struggle with depression I learned something essential. Energy, not time or money, is by far my most precious resource.

So I became a student of my own energy. And personal energy is a tricky thing to figure out. It is obviously connected to sleep, exercise, and diet. But it is also connected to things we have little or no control over, like hormones and genetics. Its calculus is utterly individual. Like weight loss (also unfortunately), its research base is n=1. You have to find out why and when you have energy and why and when you don't, both on a daily basis and on a seasonal basis. I am going to address seasonal issues in upcoming chapters, but for the rest of this one, I'm going to share some ways of the ways that I have learned to increase and protect my own energy.

FOCUS ON ONE THING

Struggling with low energy and depression is not a problem I wish on anyone. But it did teach me something very important, and its lesson is a theme that runs throughout this book: if you want to be successful over a long period of time, you must learn how to focus. Work when you are working, rest when you are resting, and don't let them bleed into one another. It turns out that my advice to focus on one thing is biblical too. I like the *God's Word* translation of Romans 12:6-8:

> God in his kindness gave each of us different gifts. If your gift is speaking what God has revealed, make sure what you say agrees with the Christian faith. If your gift is serving, then devote yourself to serving. If it is teaching, devote yourself to teaching. If it is encouraging others, devote yourself to giving encouragement. If it is sharing, be generous. If it is leadership, lead enthusiastically. If it is helping people in need, help them cheerfully.

In his immense kindness God basically told us not to try to do everything or be everything to everyone. He told us to find our gifts and devote ourselves to exercising those gifts with God's energy, which, as Paul reminds us, works so powerfully within us. The idea of devoted focus seems obvious, but it is surprising how few academics actually think about or practice devoted focus. There are a number of excellent books out there about focus, and many of them discuss how our age of distraction makes it harder and harder to practice. My favorite book on this topic is Gary Keller's *The ONE Thing: The Surprisingly Simple Truth Behind Extraordinary Results.* Although I read this book for the first time last year, its basic precepts are ones that I have followed for a long time. Keller is spot-on with his advice about the devastating consequences of mishandling your most precious resource: your energy. "Personal energy mismanagement is a silent thief of productivity," he writes.[2] To manage your energy, you must learn how to focus, and what to focus on.

If your life looks and feels more like a hopelessly tangled fishing line than a streamlined rig, you cannot afford not to read Keller's book. But since we are all busy, I'll give you my *Reader's Digest* version. Keller begins his book with a Russian proverb: "If you chase two rabbits, you will not catch either one." After years of research, Keller began to notice that successful people were the ones who were able to identify the one thing they need to accomplish to move forward in any given area, personal or vocational. The metaphor he chose to describe the energy that such focus creates is a line of dominos. The more dominoes you line up, the more energy tipping the first one creates. A tiny domino can topple dominoes more than twice its size if there are enough gradations

---

[2]Gary Keller and Jay Papasan, *The ONE Thing: The Surprisingly Simple Truth Behind Extraordinary Results* (Austin: Bard, 2013), 198.

between them. The key is determining where the lead domino is in each area and then hacking away at it until it falls.

So let's think about this idea in terms of your life as an educator. In the early years of teaching, it takes a notoriously insane amount of energy just to learn how to teach. But you also want to build your scholarly career, be present for your family, and achieve other personal goals. You might be tempted to think that the lead domino for becoming a great teacher is the amount of time you spend in preparation. But think again. This time, follow Keller's lead: "What's the ONE thing I can do such that by doing it everything else will be easier or unnecessary?" This is a very wise question. More time spent in preparation will not make everything else easier or unnecessary. More time spent grading will not make everything else easier or unnecessary. But if you think about your energy in terms of win-win that I discussed in the last chapter, the answer to Keller's question changes. The lead domino, your one thing, might be this: I am going to discover what expert teachers do in their classrooms to get the results they get. Do you see the difference? If you can topple that particular lead domino, it will set off a whole row of dominoes in your life, and your energy will increase. After you implement the strategies that are most helpful to you in different areas, the lead domino changes accordingly. Your primary mission is always to find the lead domino, the one thing. Your intelligence is not enough; it needs to be directed toward the right questions so that your energy can be spent in the best possible way, with the greatest results.

ASK QUESTIONS, CREATE HABITS

The upshot of all this is that we all must learn how to best manage our own energy, and it must begin with devoted focus. To start, I recommend asking Keller's question for all the important areas of your life and career. Initially you should limit these areas to three or four, such as teaching, scholarship, health, and family life. For example, what is the one thing I can do for my health such that by doing it everything else will be easier or unnecessary?

After you've determined your focal points, here are some other vital questions when it comes to protecting energy and time to actually do that one thing:

1. What time of day do I work best?

2. Where am I when I am the most productive?

3. What are my biggest distractions? How can I eliminate or minimize those distractions when I'm working on my one thing?

I saved a lot of time and energy when I recognized that I should never grade papers anywhere but in my office and any time but in the morning. But because mornings are the most precious time for me (I've often said that I can do almost anything before 1:00 p.m. but almost nothing after 3:00 p.m.), I have to limit the time I spend grading and be very focused when I do it. I rarely have office hours then, I never answer the phone, and, as a rule, I do not check email in the morning. This is what Keller calls time blocking, and it is essential if you are going to get your one thing done. Put this up on your office wall, and sear it into your brain: "The people who achieve extraordinary results don't achieve them by working more hours. They achieve them getting more done in the hours they work."[3]

The need for time blocking is especially true for writing, which I believe is the hardest work we do. I write best at home and only in the mornings. I have the luxury—and believe me, I know it is luxury—of having my own study. It is 7:00 a.m. on a July morning as I am writing this paragraph, and I'm in my study. To protect my

---

[3]Keller and Papasan, *ONE Thing*, 174.

one thing in this area during the academic year, I set up one or two days a week to work from home. I do not go into the office. I've scheduled this time for my one thing, so it has to be really special for me to break this date with myself. How to say no more often is the subject of my next chapter, but the short version is that you cannot learn how to say no if you aren't committed to keeping these productivity appointments with yourself. If my house is noisy that morning, I put on my noise-cancelling headphones and listen to a great internet station called Focus@Will. The station is designed by productivity experts to help listeners focus on the task they are accomplishing. It mixes up the tempo of the selections to keep your brain humming along. At the moment I am writing this, it is helping me to drown out the ubiquitous lawn mowing in my neighborhood with relaxing spa music.

After you answer these questions for yourself, then you need to get really stingy. You need to discipline yourself to set up habits that protect your energy and time. Habit is an area I love to read and think about, and I've listed a few books below to help you maximize what neuroscientists call nonconscious cognition: the thinking that goes on in the background of our conscious attention. I like to think about nonconscious cognition this way: imagine if you had to drive to work every day as a new driver. You would have to think about when to put on a blinker, how and when to brake, how far behind other cars you should be, and so on. You would spend an immense amount of energy just getting to work. But because of the power of habit, most of that activity is relegated to backseat cognition, and you can drive to work safely with a minimum of energy spent. Traffic is a different issue, but what you do every day in response to the inevitable person who cuts you off is also building a habit, for better or for worse.

All of the writers of the books I recommend below recognize that the key to productivity and self-discipline in all areas of life is to move as many difficult things as you can from conscious to nonconscious cognition. In other words, tap into the immense power of habit. One of my favorite books in this area is Charles Duhigg's *The Power of Habit*. His thesis is simple and hopeful: "Habits can be changed, if we understand how they work."[4] The first thing we must understand is that up to 40 percent of our actions are habitual, and these habits have formed and reinforced neurological patterns. The brain cannot discern the difference between a good habit and a bad one. It just follows cues and gives out rewards. But as Henry David Thoreau said, "I know of no more encouraging fact than the unquestionable ability of man to elevate his life by conscious endeavor."[5] F. M. Alexander puts it less poetically, with a contemporary twist: "People do not decide their futures, they decide their habits and their habits decide their futures."[6] Habits are powerful, and we have the ability to change them by conscious endeavor.

In addition to Duhigg's book, Kelly McGonigal's *The Willpower Instinct* is especially helpful in providing ideas of how to preserve the resource that science has proven you can exhaust through the course of your day: willpower.[7] I'll go into the limited willpower issue in chapter eight. For now I'll point out that it's important not to jump over their research to the core principles because it is the research that is the most encouraging. The research reveals that often (not always) it is not some deep spiritual problem that is

---

[4]Charles Duhigg, *The Power of Habit: Why We Do What We Do in Life and Business* (New York: Random House, 2014), xvii.

[5]Henry David Thoreau, *Walden: A Fully Annotated Edition*, ed. Jeffrey S. Cramer (New Haven: Yale University Press, 2004), 88.

[6]Quoted in Keller and Papasan, *ONE Thing*, 119.

[7]Kelly McGonigal, *The Willpower Instinct: How Self-Control Works, Why It Matters, and What You Can Do to Get More of It* (New York: Avery, 2013).

keeping you in a bad habit but a series of brain-rewarding poor choices that you made along the way that have now hardened into destructive behavior. As Duhigg explains, "This process within our brain is a three-step loop. First, there is a *cue*, a trigger that tells your brain to go into automatic mode and which habit to use. Then there is the *routine*, which can be physical or mental or emotional. Finally, there is a *reward*, which helps your brain figure out if this particular loop is worth remembering for the future."[8]

Figure 2.1. Habit loop

The brain, since it is always looking for ways to go into automatic mode, forms most habit loops quickly and easily. The little red notification number on your Facebook or email application on your smartphone is a *cue*. The *routine* is your opening the app. The *reward* is the little hit of dopamine your brain receives from the new information within the app. Pretty soon you are opening these apps without thinking at all. To change the habit, you need

[8]Duhigg, *Power of Habit*, 19.

to disrupt some part of the loop. In the above example, it is fairly easy: turn off notifications, and you remove the cue. But most of our bad habits cannot be so easily changed. The reason for this is that it is not always easy to figure out what exactly the brain is craving and why. Duhigg gives the example of a person who gets up from his desk every day at around the same time, walks out of his office, and eats a cookie. Over time, this habit is going to have some bad results. But to change this particular habit, he has to first figure out what he is actually craving and then replace the routine. In this example, the cue is the afternoon tiredness, and what the man was actually craving was distraction and a break. He could get the same reward by replacing the routine of getting a cookie with a different routine — a short walk outside or a visit with a colleague. The cue is almost impossible to alter, so what you have to replace is the routine that leads to the cookie. And then you've got to cultivate a different kind of craving, but the craving also has to be strong enough for the brain to anticipate the reward. Otherwise, it won't work.

The stories that Duhigg provides to illustrate the power of changing people's habit loops are eye-opening. Procter and Gamble at first couldn't sell Febreze, even though the product actually worked brilliantly to eliminate odors — even from skunks. They finally discovered that they needed a better reward than just removing odors, so they added a fresh scent that made people crave the feeling of cleanliness that signified the odor had been eliminated. The same with toothpaste. Americans' dental health was in decline until marketing guru Claude Hopkins figured out how to sell Pepsodent. He got people to brush their teeth not by explaining its importance to one's dental health because that was not enough of a reward to build a craving. Instead he provided the reward of a clean, fresh mouth and linking that, by advertising, to attractiveness. Sales boomed after that habit loop was established. We may be smart, but our brains are kind of stupid. They just want the rush of the reward.

Let's go back, this time with Duhigg as our guide, to our office routines. Do you have a habit of checking email first thing in the morning? This habit is giving your brain a cookie, but it is also distracting you. One professor described his epiphany after reading Duhigg's book:

> I started examining my own workflow, and when I got to the book's example of the cookie in the afternoon, I realized that checking email had become my cookie. There was a certain reward there that was throwing off my book research and writing. So I substituted taking notes on my book for checking my email, and I ended up finishing the revision of a manuscript, getting the second manuscript ready, and preparing for publication in about two months, whereas before, all of that had been taking years. Just changing one aspect of my workflow — how often I checked my email — made my personal productivity go up by at least 400 percent.[9]

I wish it were as easy for me as it was for this person, but the key is, as always, accurate self-analysis. Then you've got to work hard to find a routine and reward that your brain can anticipate. When I first discovered that I can only grade papers in the morning, I set up a weekly routine to meet a close friend for breakfast, after which we would grade together in the dining hall. That worked superbly right up until we had our first children (born around the same time), and then we just couldn't manage that commitment. So I had to find another routine and reward. I found that if, on Monday, Wednesday, and Friday mornings, I got up and out of

---

[9]Duhigg, *Power of Habit*, 284.

the house before 6:00 a.m. and went to my office to grade papers straight away, I could actually keep up with it. Your home responsibilities may not enable this kind of schedule, but the point is you have to find what works best for you given your needs. Being caught up is a superb reward, and it is another reason why I spread my writing assignments throughout the semester instead of having them turned in at the end. But by itself, the reward of being caught up was not nearly as strong as the reward of having breakfast with my friend. So I linked it to rewards that I already craved: time alone, a quiet office suite, and my favorite coffee. I added the cue and reward of subscribing to Focus@Will so that when I turn that music on, it signals to my brain that it is time to get the grading done. If I finish on time, I know I can take the reward of a chapel-time walk around the track at the football field.

A second routine I built works similarly. As a part of Wheaton's One College, One Book program, I read Bonhoeffer's *Life Together*. It convicted me that I wanted to know the whole of Scripture better than I did. So I found a great podcast and app called *The Daily Audio Bible* (DAB) where Brian Hardin, an Anglican priest, reads the Scripture every day for a year. He includes portions of the Old Testament, the New Testament, the Psalms (read through twice each year), and Proverbs. I'm on my sixth year of this habit, and it has profoundly shaped me. When I go to my office early on grading days, that is my cue. I turn on the DAB and listen as I prepare my coffee. I also use a hand grinder and pour-over method, both because it is fresher and it just feels good to perform this ritual. The coffee is a truly satisfying reward. When the Scripture ends, that is my cue that it is time to get to work. I do something similar during writing days at home. Of course my attention level varies, but the point is I'm putting myself in position to hear the Bible and then to get to work. (I also think it is especially apropos that every year, during the first or second week of class, God speaks to Job out of the whirlwind.) My husband once asked me what I got out of my habit of listening to the DAB every day, what it is that makes me want to do it—what created enough craving to make a habit. It is an excellent question, and if you understand Duhigg's habit loop, it is *the* question. My answer was that I began to crave the little bit of space that did not feel like work to me but rest. I also began to crave the joy of listening with thousands of other members of the invisible church to the Word of God. It makes me feel connected to something that God is doing right now. By nurturing the habit, I began to crave the spontaneous but God-directed collision of familiarity (the same Bible) with newness (my own situation). Now I don't think about it all. It is simply restful and soul-satisfying.

Another routine that I've set up involves my writing group. You will learn more about this group later, but since they each come into play at various point in this book, I want to refer to them by using our code names to protect the innocent. I am Hellcat. There's Kind Eyes, Hot Cross Buns, and Badass Jo, or BAJ. Hot Cross is insane about work, so I'm not surprised that she was the one who found a wonderful productivity app called *Forest*.

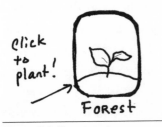

Figure 2.2. Forest app

When she introduced it to us at our breakfast meeting, we were all so excited that we all downloaded it on the spot. We now use it regularly together to spur each other on. It is based on the Pomodoro technique, whereby you set a timer for twenty-five-minute intervals, the ticking of which is supposed to remind you to stay on task for that entire segment of time. The *Forest* app simply adds more rewards: you plant your forest by staying focused for intervals that grow virtual trees on your virtual field. If you look at your phone, it will give you a message like "Put down your phone!" If you do something else with your phone, your tree dies, which is freakishly disturbing. You can also compete with your friends on a daily basis. The one who plants the highest number of focused minutes becomes queen of the forest for the day. Our competition is healthy. We encourage one another, and we don't trash talk, except in good fun. At this particular moment, I'm Queen Hellcat because I already have four beautiful Wisteria trees in my forest, and it is 10:30 a.m. (Night owls will catch me later on, no doubt.) BAJ's daughter got so excited when her mother ruled the forest that she drew a picture of it for her. (BAJ is known to her daughter as "Best Artist Jo," by the way).

Forest also allows friends to create and join in a virtual field together, in which the health of the forest depends on everyone

Figure 2.3. Queen of the forest by Annelise

staying on task. It is surprisingly effective. Apparently you can also use your gold coin rewards to plant an actual tree, but I haven't tried this yet.

Follow Keller's lead for each area of your life and work that matters to you. What's the one habit that you can build this September, such that by building it, everything else becomes easier and unnecessary? Do it!

FOR ADDITIONAL ENCOURAGEMENT

Delbanco, Andrew. *College: What It Was, Is, and Should Be.* Princeton: Princeton University Press, 2014.

I wish every administrator would take the time to read this book. Delbanco understands why our students actually go to college—even when they themselves don't know it yet. They go for the transformative experience, "It is a pipe dream to imagine that every student can have the sort of experience that our richest colleges, at their best, provide. But it is a nightmare society that affords the chance to learn and grow only to the wealthy, brilliant, or lucky few. Many remarkable teachers in America's community colleges, unsung private colleges, and underfunded public colleges live this truth every day, working to keep the ideal of democratic education alive" (7-8). We need to be able to articulate why we do what we do in order to stay inspired to teach.

Duhigg, Charles. *The Power of Habit: Why We Do What We Do in Life and Business.* New York: Random House, 2014.

As I mentioned above, Duhigg's book is filled with stories that will make you think twice about what you do and why. Don't skip over the research and examples.

Keller, Gary, and Jay Papasan. *The ONE Thing: The Surprisingly Simple Truth Behind Extraordinary Results.* Austin: Bard, 2013.

BAJ is kind of annoyed with this book because it assumes a male breadwinner's luxury of having the possibility for uninterrupted time. She certainly has a point. But this doesn't change its essential truth: if you want to get things done, you have to create time when you can focus. See chapter five if you have difficulty creating spaces of time for focus. If you are a mom of young children, be patient during these years that you won't be able to plant as much as you'd like to. I'll address this issue later.

Rubin, Gretchen. *Better Than Before: What I Learned About Making and Breaking Habits—to Sleep More, Quit Sugar, Procrastinate Less, and Generally Build a Happier Life.* New York: Broadway, 2015.

Rubin is a practical thinker and a very encouraging writer. This book convinced my husband to eliminate a couple of bad habits and start several good ones. I can hear you opening your Amazon app right now.

3

October

Women in the No:
Say No in Order to Say Yes

When I began my college teaching career in 1999, I was one of very few women on the faculty. There wasn't even a maternity leave policy in place. It turns out that I was also early evidence of a big change that was on the way. Many more women were hired in the years right after me, most of them with young children or about to have them. Needless to say, the culture of the college was not quite ready for us.

One of the women who arrived two years after me was a young scholar I'll call Angela. Angela was great for the rest of us single folk because she poured a lot of her substantial energy into creating social gatherings. I met my future husband at one of these gatherings, so I am especially grateful to Angela. But the best thing she did was to help women on the faculty to understand their need to learn to say no. She even started an alternative "power table" in the lunchroom called "Women in the No": WiN. This move was so edgy at the time that I remember thinking that it took an act of courage even to be loosely associated with this group. I don't know what ultimately happened to this effort (I rarely eat in the dining hall), but I expect it just kind of dissolved over time.

Women faculty often just have too much to do to be in social groups for very long.

What women quickly discover when they arrive on campus is that if you have minority status of any sort, you get called on more often to do everything. This is not all bad, of course. We can all agree that we desperately need the point of view of women and other minorities when it comes to institutional decisions. This became especially clear to me one year when I discovered that our faculty personnel committee—literally the face of the college to potential new hires—was about to consist of only men if we weren't strategic about preventing it. But the curse is that faculty personnel committee is one of the most time- and energy-intensive of all commitments, and one I would not wish on anyone. Thus a few dilemmas are created. Should I nominate a fellow female colleague when I know that this will be a huge time commitment for her? If I get nominated, should I say yes? Can I say no? Should I?

These questions are compounded by a young faculty member's pre-tenure status. Many new faculty members want to be, and want to be seen as, team players. In the case of Wheaton and many other liberal arts colleges, they also know that institutional service is one of four "promotable strengths," supposedly on par with teaching, scholarship, and student mentoring. This situation is further compounded by the evidence that female faculty are often expected to serve more and will be judged more harshly than male faculty for appearing unwilling to fill service roles.[1] Regardless, since service is important and time-consuming, we all, men and women alike, must learn to be especially shrewd.

---

[1] It is not my purpose here to don my scholarly hat and give links to this data, but interested parties should consult the ongoing bibliography kept by Danica Savonick and Cathy N. Davidson, "Gender Bias in Academe: An Annotated Bibliography of Important Recent Studies," HASTAC, 2015, www.hastac.org/blogs/superadmin/2015/01/26/gender-bias-academe-annotated-bibliography-important-recent-studies.

When it comes to navigating this difficult terrain, Gretchen Rubin has done a great service by identifying what she calls the "four tendencies" of all people.[2] Like me, Rubin is one of those people who can't get enough of Meyers-Briggs, Enneagram, and other classification systems, primarily because self-knowledge is key to thriving in this world. Rubin has observed that people tend to be either Obligers, Questioners, Upholders, or Rebels. As I've looked at myself and the people around me, I think she is on to something here. In my inner circle of friends at the college (the women in my writing group; see chapter eleven), we have one Obliger, one Upholder, and two Questioners. Rebels would have a hard time at a place like Wheaton. In my experience as an academic, Obligers are usually (but certainly not always) women. They are the ones who do everything that is asked of them simply because it asked of them. They think of themselves in terms of serving others. And, of course, this is a good thing, as it is very close to the kind of self-emptying love that Christ himself commanded of us. But Obligers also have the hardest time saying no and are the most likely to spread themselves thin to the point of dissolution. Questioners are very nearly the opposite of Obligers. They will gladly do things that make sense to them to do but will question the validity of any other demands placed on their time. Upholders and Rebels are more rare. Upholders are those that are motivated by their own internal commitments (like Questioners) but also feel especially committed to doing what must be done for the sake of the institution. Like Obligers, they also can get incredibly burned out if they cannot learn to say no. Rebels, born to say no, have far less of a problem with burnout.

I am obviously a Questioner, and in this area of my life, it has served me well. If you are an Obliger or an Upholder, trust me here:

---

[2]Gretchen Rubin, *The Four Tendencies: The Indispensable Personality Profiles That Reveal How to Make Your Life Better* (New York: Harmony, 2017).

you really need to learn how to say no. You need to know both when and why to say it if you want to flourish in this profession.

Let's start with the why first. The main reason why all of us need to learn to say no is that we are finite human beings in a world with an endless amount of stuff to be done. Other people, especially employers, will load us down with as many things to do as we will agree to accept. This is not personal, as if administrators are seeking you out to load you like a pack mule. It is just a fact of life that in every single organization of which you are a part, there is always more that can be done. Understanding the impersonal nature of this reality is essential to being able to say no. You simply do not have the time or the capacity to do all of the things that could be asked of you, and you need to respect that about yourself. Full stop.

But there is another reason why learning to say no is an essential skill for educators in particular. Gary Keller, the wise writer of *The ONE Thing* I introduced you to in the last chapter, explains that "the art of saying yes is, by default, the art of saying no. Saying yes to everyone is the same as saying yes to nothing."[3] Let's unpack this brilliant idea a little. Remember that Keller's advice is for all of us to find the one thing that is most needed in any given area and say a big, hearty, disciplined and habitual yes to that. If I've discovered that the one thing I need to get my book done is at least one day a week of working from home, I must say no to anything that is asked of me that will contaminate that plan. Saying yes to my one thing is utterly dependent on my ability to say no, potentially, to a large number of other worthy things. In short, we must learn how to say yes in order to say no, and no in order to say yes.

---

[3] Gary Keller and Jay Papasan, *The ONE Thing: The Surprisingly Simple Truth Behind Extraordinary Results* (Austin: Bard, 2013), 192.

SAY YES IN ORDER TO SAY NO

This is easier said than done, even for Questioners. Most people, especially Christians, want to help out when asked. So what can be done about this? I have found that it is easier to say no when I think of my own plan as an unbreakable appointment that I have made with myself. The trick is to learn how to say yes to ourselves first, and this will give us power to say no to other things. In my writing group, we have made a pact that we will ask the other group members for input before deciding whether to agree to do something that is not a part of our employment contracts. The Upholder and the Obliger have the hardest time with this. I have an animated GIF that I repeatedly send to them via text message: a white cat in a ridiculous hat, rolling her head in a sassy fashion, with bold text that flashes "O HELL NO!" This is also why I've earned the code name Hellcat. Even if you do not have difficulty saying no, I strongly suggest you set up this kind of support system. We all need to remember why we have said yes to the things we have said yes to. When those things are a little harder to immediately quantify—like being home with family, our own scholarly projects, and just plain old time to read—we have to work harder to build a system that will protect the yes.

That is one way in which saying yes gives you the ability to say no. The other is equally important: say yes, but do so strategically. We must learn *when* to say yes. It is simply not fair or ethical, for example, for any faculty member to repeatedly refuse institutional work that will always fall, as a result, on the shoulders of others. This also becomes the curse of Obligers, who are keenly aware of exactly this injustice. At the beginning of my career, I was unmarried and had more time on my hands. I wisely surmised that this wouldn't necessarily always be the case, so I readily agreed to serve on committees that interested me the most. I served on the

English department search committee both because it interested me and because I wanted to be a team player. I had a number of years to try to get some good work in and earn the right of refusal later. The best yes I said was to serving on one of the largest and busiest faculty committees, the curriculum and educational policies committee. I was elected to this committee right after I got married, knowing that we would try to get pregnant sooner rather than later. And sure enough, I was in my third and final year of service when I got pregnant. I was able to say no for a while after that in part because I had an infant but mostly because I had earned it. Years later, when I was thinking about going up for promotion, I said yes to the most difficult (and most interesting) committee — faculty personnel — which gave me the right to say no to all difficult committee work for a few years after that. Those polite refusals were huge, for they led directly to my second published book. In short, I said yes in a timely way to something that was not all that important to me in order to protect my ability to say yes to something that was.

I know that I risk the ire of Obligers and Upholders (and administrators) when I give this kind of advice. If you feel peeved by my perspective, it can be productive to ask yourself why. Do you envy me for having courage to stand up for myself? Or is it that you haven't identified your one thing, and it feels good to do everything that is asked of you? Do you feel that working at a Christian institution means that you should give more of yourself to your job, even when it would take you away from your family or church? Why do you feel that way? Self-knowledge is indispensable in this area. As I mentioned earlier, I have always struggled with low amounts of personal energy, so for me to agree to do something too demanding for my schedule is to risk something more than just my time. It is to risk my joy. The more people-intensive demands that are placed on me, the more tired I get. The more tired I get, the more I lose control of things I know I need like exercise, time alone, and sleep. Those things are critical to me being the kind of person I want to be when I am with my students and my family: loving, attentive, inspired, and inspiring. So for me, saying no is a vital part of my obedience to God and my commitment to my vocation.

GET THINGS DONE

We all want to be able to say yes to things that are important to us to do, and to have the time and energy to do them well. My own ability to do so was profoundly altered by one thing: the day I finally discovered a personal organization system that works. Oddly enough, the breakthrough came right after the birth of my son. While some parents see their lives get thrown into utter chaos after the birth of their first child, I actually became more productive and more organized.

Let me be clear: this did not happen overnight. I was so overwhelmed by caring for a baby that I remember actually thinking that I would never be able to read a book from beginning to end again. I have told and retold this story to a number of colleagues who are new mothers because it speaks to a reality that we must get our minds around: different seasons of our lives require different things. As many others have said, "This, too, shall pass." Like all profound truths, it seems obvious, but it is difficult to internalize. As I will discuss in the next chapter, I have an especially hard time remembering, when I am ill or in a tough situation, that this is not my new reality.

So how did I get more organized and productive when I returned to work after having a baby? First, having fallen into a deep postpartum depression, I learned that I had been depressed for a very long time. Depression is funny like that. How do you identify something as abnormal when it is all that you have ever known? I knew that I did not have the same amount of energy as most other people. I knew that I had to exercise all the time to get my serotonin levels going. But I had no idea how much energy was required just to struggle against my lack of energy. When I hit my postpartum nadir, I got help, and it helped more than I could have imagined.

That key change gave me just enough energy to discover an approach to life organization that works for me: David Allen's *Getting Things Done*, known by fans as GTD.[4] Oddly enough, the book is incredibly disorganized and hard to read, but to give Allen credit, it is not an easy system to explain to others. But his approach completely changed my life. I hope my *Reader's Digest* version will be helpful. I modified his system to fit an academic career, and I'm always looking for more hacks, as you will soon see. This section will be a bit laborious if you do not want to change your organizational system right now. If this describes you, I will not be offended if you skip all of this and move on to the next chapter. But whether you read this section or not, the most important thing to remember is the purpose of building a workable system. The purpose is not to be efficient for the sake of efficiency, or to be able to do more. The purpose is to be able to draw a line between your work life and your home life. Get things done efficiently so that you can be more than just someone who gets things done.

The good news is that following his system does not require fancy equipment. All you need is:

1. A calendar, onto which you only write time-sensitive events, never projects or steps.

---

[4]David Allen and James Fallows, *Getting Things Done: The Art of Stress-Free Productivity*, rev. ed. (New York: Penguin, 2015).

2. Some sort of organization tool that will help you manage several different to-do lists. I use an application called *Things*, but you can also use an actual notebook (with dividers) and pen, which is what I did at first when I was learning the system.

3. An inbox (including email inbox) designed to be empty at the end of each day.

The first thing to understand about Allen's system is that its primary purpose is to help you offload all the "stuff" that you have to do that clogs your brain and drains your energy. You offload this stuff by having a reliable system of capturing and organizing it so you don't have to worry about it. Allen uses the vague word *stuff* on purpose, because the stuff that hits us in life has all different kinds of ontological statuses. There's the driveway that needs a sealcoat. The fact you haven't figured out life insurance. The hundred-plus unanswered emails (not anymore if you follow this system). The book review you promised for that journal. The nagging suspicion you need to spend more time with your children. Your prayer life could use work. Do you see why this can only be termed vaguely as *stuff*? It comes at us like this, poured into the giant inboxes of our lives.

Allen's genius is this: the traditional to-do list method fails because it is chaotic. It also does not identify the actual Next Action Step. Nobody can have one big to-do list for all of the things we actually want to get done, especially when they are as vague as "spend more time with my children." Instead, you need to figure out:

1. What the thing means to you.

2. What the actual Next Action Step on it is.

3. Where you physically are when you take that kind of action.

These three determinations are at the core of Allen's decision tree.

When the thought comes to you that you need to "figure out your life insurance," that is "stuff." The first step is to ask what that particular thing means to you. If you decide you need to do this multi-step thing sooner rather than later, it becomes a project. After you determine whether or not it is actionable (yes) and requires more than two minutes to complete (yes), the tree leads you to the question, "What is the next action?" This step is at the heart of Allen's system. The most important decision you make is determining and capturing (on the correct list) what the actual

Figure 3.1. GTD decision tree

Next Action Step is. Have you ever been working on a manuscript when it pops into your mind that you need to call the dentist? That's what he wants to avoid. So Allen says you need to put any to-do action that you cannot immediately complete into a list that is set up according to *where you are and when it is that you can most efficiently do these kinds of things* (which is not in the middle of writing). I keep track of these areas in an application called *Things*. This is the same "things" in *Getting Things Done* because the software was designed for fans of Allen's system. *Things* syncs across all of my devices, so I always have it with me. My *Things* has the following main Areas, which are effectively separate to-do lists:

1. Writing

2. Wheaton

3. Home/Online

4. Errands

5. Agenda

6. Phone

7. Someday/Maybe

Things and other applications feature a place where you can list your projects as well as all the steps you will need to complete them, but I hardly ever use this feature. I find it easier to just immediately determine and record the actual Next Action Step and record it in the area where I would be when I do it.

Let's see how Next Action Steps end up on one of the seven location-keyed lists above. When I'm grading papers or writing or doing some other real work and the random thought comes into my head like, *I need to call the dentist,* I create the action item "Call the dentist" under Phone in my *Things* app. Then I go back to work. When I've steeled myself up enough to make phone calls, there it will be. I make all my phone calls at once, and I'm much happier. By the way, if you don't have a dentist yet, then "Call the dentist" is not a Next Action Step. Instead, that would be "Ask my local Facebook contacts for dentist recommendations." In my system, that would become a to-do in my *Things* app in area three, Home/Online. Similarly, if the next step for the book review I agreed to write was "Read *Title of Boring Academic Book*," I would put that on my Writing list. When I saw this Next Action Step, I would know which project it was for.

The key to Allen's system is that you properly identify the actual Next Action Step. It's so important that he capitalizes the three words. The psychological release comes from putting all of the "stuff" you encounter where it belongs in the system so that the system carries it around, not you. When it occurs to me that my driveway needs a sealcoat, the decision tree leads me to locate what the actual Next Action Step would be *for me*, which might be "Go online to find two companies willing to give quotes." I would put that step in the area Home/Online, because that is where I do stuff like that. The next step would not be "sealcoat the driveway" unless I was planning to do it myself, and even then, the actual Next Action Step would be "purchase sealcoating equipment," which would go under Errands. See the logic of the system? Remember that the Areas in *Things* or your to-do notebook are lists that are organized around when and where you are when you do certain things. It is not useful to write down "Purchase sealcoating equipment" on a random piece of paper when you are at your desk at work. But it is useful to have it in a list of errands you already have down because of where you are when you do errands: out and about.

In my case, sealcoating the driveway is something that my husband has agreed to be in charge of. So when I notice that the driveway needs a coat and it pops into my mind in the annoying way these things always do, I do not make a project out of it. Instead, I put my Next Action Step in the "Agenda" area of my *Things* app: "Ask Steve about sealcoating the drive." Agenda items are those that involve delegating or discussing things with other people. Boom! Sealcoating is now off my mind until I do my weekly review, which occurs a day before my weekly meeting with my husband. I'll see the action item and say to myself, *Ah, I need to ask Steve as non-naggingly as possible when he is planning to get the sealcoating taken care of.* Whew.

You can also easily see at this point why a weekly review process is essential. If you write all these things down and never look at them, they are useless. Allen recommends a weekly review of all areas and projects every Friday afternoon and that you should schedule this as a regularly recurring item on your calendar. Although I am often exhausted at that particular time, there is wisdom in this advice. It is remarkably invigorating to leave your office for the weekend with a clean desk and an empty inbox.

If you have not been following Allen's system and have a lot of stuff in your mind and all over your desk, getting caught up will take a very long time and a lot of energy, so clear out an entire day (or more) for it. When you are caught up, staying caught up is key. Here's a very brief primer on how to get to the elusive land of "caught up." First collect all of your "stuff" in one big physical inbox (a pile). If you do this step correctly, the big pile will include things like those picture hangers you bought but haven't used and are now cluttering your desk. It also includes a brainstorm list about what projects are on your mind but you haven't done anything about yet. Get it all down, and don't leave anything out. The second step is the hard part. You must follow the decision tree for *every single item* (fig. 3.1.). Allen recommends that you look at each thing and ask, "What is it?" and especially, "What does this mean to *me*?" This is brilliant because you will not be able to know what to do with the thing unless you know what it means to you. Then follow the tree to some conclusion: discard; do; defer; or delegate. The very first time you do this, you will also have to create Next Action Steps (organized by area) galore. This is very hard work. Take frequent breaks. Breathe. You will have to do this at home and again at your office, so give yourself some grace!

I keep a copy of Allen's decision tree on my door in my study if I need a refresher. Let's put it to work. Let's say you got a flyer advertising your college's glee club concert. This is not actionable for you if you're uninterested or busy that evening. Recycle the flyer. But if you were interested in going (you enjoy glee club concerts and are thinking about it), it is actionable. So you must immediately ask the question, "What's the Next Action Step?" And here again is Allen's genius: the very next question on the decision tree is "Will it take less than two minutes?" If the answer is yes, then *do it right now!* The reason for this is obvious—the time and energy to file such a thing for later is not worth it. In this case it definitely does take less than two minutes to do something with it: you put the event on your calendar or write it on your agenda list (if you want to confer with your husband about going).

Why does Allen's system seem so simple right now, like when your high school teacher did calculus problems on the chalkboard, but you came home and couldn't do them? It's because I haven't talked about the biggest inbox of all: email. Allen helps us to understand why folks end up with thousands of emails cluttering their inbox. If emails were just letters from friends (like they were in the blissful early days of email), you would sit down and write responses when you had the chance. But that is not what email is today. An email inbox is just a big messy inbox for our whole lives—not just for work or home or family and friends, but for all of it. An email is sometimes information, sometimes a work request, sometimes correspondence, and sometimes material you need to do work on or defer or keep for reference. That's a lot of stuff. What does your inbox look like right now? Is it impossible? If you are just starting out on GTD, it is probably a good idea just to put all of it into your archive folder and start again with a new folder system as I describe it below.

The reason email is in a special category for twenty-first-century knowledge workers is because it has replaced paper support items for most of us in almost every project area. In other words, most people want to keep various emails for reference or need to defer the emails until they are able to respond to them. Since that is the case, I use my Outlook inbox as a partial mirror of my *Things* database. The difference is that my email is (ideally) primarily used to store reference materials or things that I have *already acted on* in some way (by delegating, deferring, or doing).

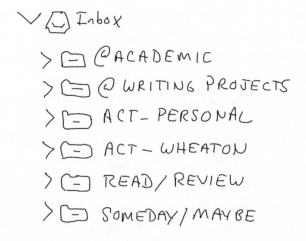

Figure 3.2. My Outlook inbox

If you don't have rules set up for first-level, automatic email processing, do that now. Take the time to learn how Rules work. It is more than worth it. I automatically direct certain types of emails to folders called ACT-WHEATON and ACT-PERSONAL and (try to) process those emails once a day. This means that my Rules automatically send my primary email to one of three email inboxes: the main one and the two above. I do this so that when I get an email from Amazon or my son's school district, I won't be distracted by it while I'm at work. Even with all these rules diverting my email automatically and a separate Gmail account for junky commercial stuff (essential), my primary inbox is still flooded daily.

Have you set up your email rules? If not, stop reading now and do it — I'll wait.[5]

My main folders, ACT-WHEATON and ACT-PERSONAL, also have project subfolders under each of them where I keep reference emails that have *already been processed (done, deferred, or delegated) by me.* For example, a current subfolder in my ACT-WHEATON is called SPCC Committee, which is a strategic planning committee I'm on. I use the subfolder to keep communications from this committee, and I will keep this folder here until the committee's work is complete. I use this subfolder as a *temporary* holding place for work I need to do for the committee, making sure to put the Next Action Step on my *Things* app so that it doesn't

---

[5]I'm being dramatic here because usually the best way to set up rules if you haven't been using them properly is to delete any you may have already set up and start afresh. This means that every future email you get, you will have to set up a rule to have it automatically sent to no more than three inboxes. This will take weeks but will pay off in the end. I have ACT-WHEATON and ACT-PERSONAL, which captures emails that I have directed to be sent there. I look at these inboxes, and of course my primary inbox, at least once a day. I also have a subfolder called COMMERCIAL that I automatically send stuff that doesn't need a reply, like receipts, and a READ/REVIEW for listservs or similar items.

get lost. The Next Action Step might be "Respond to the latest proposal," which I received as an attachment. (That's why I want to keep the email in a subfolder where I can find it when I'm ready to do that kind of work.) The @WRITING and @ACADEMIC do not receive any email forwarded automatically by Rules. You do not want to have unread email diverted to too many places, or you will lose track of it. Instead, these folders contain only project sub-folders for reference items. When I get invited to give a keynote lecture and accept it, for example, I make a project subfolder in Outlook under the area @ACADEMIC. Most project subfolders in my "Academic" folder in Outlook are named by the date and place of the event. Any emails I get about this event go into this folder *after I have acted on them*, where I can easily retrieve them. Remember that an email is not a Next Action Step. Don't put an email in a subfolder until you have processed it in some way.

Let's flesh this out a bit more. At this particular moment I've got seven academic projects I'm working on. One of them is speaking at a Lilly conference at Central College. So in Outlook under @ACADEMIC, I currently have a subfolder named "2017.10 Lilly-Central." All the communications regarding this conference are filed in this folder for easy retrieval. When I get an email from the organizer of the conference asking me to go ahead and book my flight, I immediately put the to-do item "Book flight to Iowa" in my *Things* app, in my case, under Home/Online. That is where I do such things, and I know it will be there when I'm ready to do things like book flights. Then I reply (if necessary) and move his email to the relevant subfolder (where I keep it for reference only). Thus the email is fully processed, even though I haven't done the action yet. To give another example about the importance of determining the Next Action Step, it would be beyond meaningless for me to put on my *Things* app to-do list "Write the Lilly speech," because that is not really a Next Action Step. A Next Action Step would be something like "Look over the invitation email and think about what I most want to say" or "email the organizer my title." In truth, I don't feel it is necessary to write down most of my Next Action Steps for this kind of project, but if I needed to do so for any given project, I know exactly *where* I would do so: on the *Things* app under whatever area best fits.

So let's open your email with David Allen. Let's pretend you are all caught up, have Rules and project subfolders place, and you are receiving new emails only. I will repeat this fact later, but the earlier you can learn that you should not open your email until you are ready to process all of it, the better. *Process* does not necessarily mean *answer*. I strongly advise that you not receive email on your phone and that you process email only once or twice a day (and not during your best energy hours). If you have a supervisor who cannot deal with this, make sure they know that you are not being irresponsible or unavailable but that you are trying to focus on real work when you are at work. Try to figure out some other arrangement for real emergencies. Most of the time people just have to learn that you have more to do than to sit in front of your email waiting for it to ding. And by the way, make sure you turn off all such dings, as they are definitely productivity killers.

You have your coffee, and you are ready to process. You open your mail, and the first one is from a student turning in a paper. This is definitely important, definitely actionable, and definitely takes longer than two minutes to complete. But because you have a system in place, this is easy—you defer the grading by filing the attachment (the student paper) where you put all such things until you are ready to do them. Then you send a standard response (I got your paper, thanks!) and archive the email. Thus, the email is processed and put away, though the work it represents is not yet done. By the way, I use the app Notability to assess student papers digitally, which I organize in a file called "To Grade." This works very well because I then have a copy of the paper in case I forget to record the grade or something else happens.

You next email contains a document that you need to review for a committee that you are on. This is trickier because it is important (you should do it) and actionable (you can do it), but it will take longer than two minutes of your time. It also doesn't fit easily into an established workflow like grading papers does. In this particular case, I would create a Next Action Step — "review the X committee document" — in the Wheaton area in my *Things* app (because I would only do this kind of work at my office) and maybe put a deadline on it so that it appears in my notifications as the deadline draws nearer. Since I will need this information later, I would then move the email with its attachment into a project subfolder under ACT-WHEATON that I had created for that particular committee. In my weekly review, I would (ideally) catch it and then make sure to make time (ideally) to actually do it.

Your next email is a news notice about things that are going on around the college this week. You look at it, put any events you want to go to on your calendar, and archive it in case you want to retrieve it. And on you go.

Once you start processing stuff using Allen's decision tree, it easily becomes a habit. The psychological release then frees you up to spend more time thinking about why you do what you do and to consider doing some of the things you have filed under Someday/Maybe. The important thing is tweaking the system until it works for you and never forgetting to do the weekly review. If you want to read another brief description of the nitty gritty of Allen's system, Cal Newport has a blog called Study Hacks with a

very useful post called "A Whirlwind Tour of Getting Things Done."
At the end of his post, he summarizes the system as follows:

1. Get all of the stuff in your life out of your mind and into
   collection bins.

2. Process these bins at least once a day.

3. During the day, use your calendar and next actions list to
   help decide what to do next.

4. Once a week, clean up your system and check in on your
   projects list.

5. Every few months reflect on the big picture questions in your
   life, and make sure these are reflected in your projects and
   next actions list.

If you process your stuff daily, it is never overwhelming, and
your weekly review is a piece of cake. You just look over your projects
and next action steps and see where you are. Voila—everything's
peachy! Right?

Sort of. Astute readers will notice that there is a significant catch
to the GTD system. How you respond to this catch will determine
how useful GTD is for you. The catch is this: processing all the
"stuff" that most educators get every day is very, very difficult. It
often involves high-level decision making that is mentally and
psychologically taxing.

Let me put myself on the chopping block to show you what I
mean. As I'm writing this, it is the afternoon. Since I've already accomplished my one thing for the day (writing), I'm going to check
my email and open the door to its onslaught of demands. (Thing
9: Willpower is a limited resource. Don't waste it on email.) Lo and
behold, among many other things I see this subject line: "Invitation
from the Alumni Association." It turns out to be a request from the

director of the alumni association to speak briefly to the board of directors about an alumni faculty development grant I received to go to Europe last summer. I could not have planned a more perfect example for us. This is exactly why our email gets backed up in the first place. It is difficult to decide about things like this because I don't want to think about that right now. This is someone asking me for some of my precious time this fall to talk to strangers—and on a Saturday morning too! But the fact is that I am very grateful to the alumni board for giving me these funds, so I also want to do it. If I'm an Obliger or an Upholder, I know I will say yes, so the best thing to do is reply immediately, put it on the calendar, delete the email or archive it for reference, and move on. Waiting around to reply in this case would only hurt me and hurt the director by keeping her in suspense. But I'm a Questioner, and so a tug-of-war has started inside me. It is the tug-of-war that keeps me from processing this email immediately.

Here is my problem, naked to the wind for everyone to see. My email inbox becomes a holding ground for decisions that I can't or won't make. For me to grow in this area I need to force myself to make hard decisions on the spot. Deferring a *decision* is not the same thing as deferring an *action*. The latter is okay, but the former is not. If it is clearly a lower priority item, I could shuffle it to a generic folder (like ACT-WHEATON), but most of the time that's just a delay strategy. Stuff often goes there to die. So, reader, should I say yes to this request right now?

Drum roll . . . I did. I replied yes to the email, put the item on my calendar, deleted the email, and felt virtuous for following my own advice. And I responded much more quickly than most people would, which was appreciated by the organizer. For me to stay caught up with email, I need enough self-awareness to know that at the end of the day, my gratitude for the alumni association grant exceeds my introverted desire to stay home on Saturday morning. What I hope you will see in this example is the importance of identifying what is actually causing the email log jam. For me it is most often a matter of not being able to choose what I know is the lesser pain. Most of the time I flip through my email and ignore stuff that bugs me and hope that it goes away. But the pain I am choosing by not making a decision is usually much worse than just doing the dang thing. Because, as Allen insists, I won't be able to actually get it off of my mind until I do. So it is time for me to sear my own mantra on my forehead: *I will not open my email unless and until I am truly ready to process everything that comes into it!*

With this decision made, I feel psychologically empowered to tackle the rest of my inbox. I'm on a roll! Luckily my next several emails are easier: a notice from the library about overdue items. Does it take me less than two minutes to log on and renew the books? Yes, it does. So I do it. Delete. Next, a shipping confirmation from Amazon, which I keep in business. First, I set up the rule I should have already set up for these items (what's this thing doing in my main inbox?), then delete. The rule I set up is for the Amazon confirmations to all go to a subfolder COMMERCIAL, but I could just as easily send them to the trash or the main archive, because they are not necessary for me to review. One of the things I've learned about email management is that using the main archive folder is better than creating a lot of little ones. It takes less time to file random reference items and is fully searchable. As I mentioned above, I do set up subfolders for project support items (like the keynote addresses) because I need to find some such items quickly and easily.

Next, there's a note from someone in my small group from church reminding me of a meeting. I make sure the meeting is on my calendar, reply if I want, and delete. Then there's an email from a friend about plans to shower her husband with cards for his fiftieth birthday. I create a Next Action Step in *Things* (send a birthday card to Scott) and move the email to my main archive in case I need to find the original instructions again. And so on. The more you do this kind of processing daily, the easier each day becomes. My inbox is empty again. Whew.

I want to say one quick other word about email before I end this chapter. If you are an administrator, you will have to deal with email more frequently than most academics do, but you should still endeavor to not let it rule your life or dictate the structure of your days. Because email is such a random inbox, it can really divide and conquer you if you don't have a good strategy for managing it. If you are a high school teacher who gets regular email from parents, you might want to set aside certain times of your day when you deal with that, and only that, to keep it from getting out of hand. In all these things you have to protect your "real" work time and find the system that does the best job for you.

When I actually follow Allen's system, it works superbly. By now you see that it is not foolproof (mostly because fools like me are using it), but if you are able to take some time to make it your own, it will help clear your head of the stuff that keeps popping into it. It will help you say yes more often to the real work that you want to spend your time doing, like meeting with students. You will be better able to assess how important certain requests are to you, say no when it isn't the right time, and say yes when it is. And that is what it is all about.

FOR ADDITIONAL ENCOURAGEMENT

Allen, David, and James Fallows. *Getting Things Done: The Art of Stress-Free Productivity.* Rev. ed. New York: Penguin, 2015.

Classic. If you have even a slight inkling toward following Allen's system, this book is indispensable.

Csikszentmihalyi, Mihaly. *Flow: The Psychology of Optimal Experience*. New York: Harper, 2008.

This book helped me to understand why people are actually happier when they are in a state of flow at work than they are when watching television or other mindless amusements. We should be grateful for the meaningful work we do rather than always trying to get it out of the way.

Newport, Cal. *Deep Work: Rules for Focused Success in a Distracted World*. New York: Grand Central, 2018.

I love this book. Newport argues that because of ubiquitous digital distractions, knowledge workers are losing the ability to do the deep work that our professions require. "A 2012 McKinsey study found that the average knowledge worker now spends more than 60 percent of the workweek engaged in electronic communication and Internet searching, with close to 30 percent of a worker's time dedicated to reading and answering e-mail" (6). Successful people are those that can say no to these distractions and return to the deep.

Sparks, David. *Email: A MacSparky Field Guide*. Available in iBooks.

If email is creating a productivity problem, this book can help. The main thing I learned from Sparks is to have a primary archive folder and use subfolders more sparingly.

November

Early Onset Winter

L ike everyone else in America over a certain age, I will never forget where I was and what I was doing on the morning of September 11, 2001. Things had just gotten underway in earnest for my third year of teaching at Wheaton, and I was feeling pretty good about my life overall. It was a beautiful day. The air was football-season crisp, and the sky was blue. Since it was Tuesday, I was working from home. I had just discovered that my adopted feral kitten, Principessa, had peed in my gym bag when my phone rang. It was a friend, who told me to turn on the television. What I did next was what many others did that day: watched, prayed, cried, and talked with loved ones.

When I returned to campus the next morning, it was very difficult to know what to do. We were all numb. When we heard that one of our alumni, Todd Beamer, was on the plane that crashed in Pennsylvania, it added a personal layer of grief for our community. Wheaton is a Midwestern college with students from all over the world, so some of them knew others who lost their lives that day too. When something like this happens, most faculty members know that it will not and cannot be business as usual. We know that we must help students to process. We know that we need time and space to process too.

I don't remember what I did in my classes that Wednesday, but I know it wasn't about literature. I remember inviting students to stay and talk if they wanted to, or leave if they wanted to. That was fine for Wednesday, but what about Friday? It was so difficult to figure out when to return to the syllabus. To complicate things even more, a national event of grief is one of those things that hits people in very different ways. Some students could not concentrate at all, but others needed the distraction of getting back to some kind of normalcy in the classroom. I'm sure I made lots of mistakes, but I did the best I could.

ADJUST EXPECTATIONS

I'm beginning this chapter with 9/11 because of what I learned about its impact on me. Although I didn't discern it at the time, it cast a deep shadow over what is normally the most energizing part of the academic year for me. It was, in short, an early onset winter. As the weeks progressed into actual winter, I found myself in a deep depression. I was single at the time, and I began to withdraw from many of the social events I used to enjoy. What I needed was to give myself as much grace as I was trying to give the students. Just because grief isn't personal doesn't mean it's not enervating. But I did not understand that then.

Of course I could not predict that fifteen years later, it would be personal and centered in my department. This time it was November, a few weeks before Thanksgiving. One of my friends and most brilliant of colleagues, Brett Foster, had been fighting cancer for over a year, and everyone knew he was near the end of his life. He died at home on a Monday night, during one of the performances that our student theater group had put together featuring many of his poems. I got the text while my husband and I were watching the Chicago Bears play Monday Night Football, which is something that Brett had often joined us at our house to do. Steve and I wept and said to each other that this is not right. Brett should have been at our house watching the game — not dying! The next night many of us faculty from different departments gathered together at one of Brett's closest friend's house. It was the right thing to do, and I am grateful that he opened his home to us that night. We cried and shared stories and were just together. Not surprisingly, Wednesday was a very numb day in all of my classes. I happened to be teaching on Emily Dickinson, so all I remember about that day was how much the poem "After great pain, a formal feeling comes — " took on a deeper resonance for all of us. Poetry did provide some healing salve.

On Friday morning I was in my office early and still very dazed. Although I'm always in the office early on Friday mornings, on this day my heart hurt because I knew I would be going to my friend's visitation that afternoon and his funeral the next day. As I was thinking about this, I heard someone weeping outside my door. I remember thinking that a former student must have just received the news of Brett's death when I got a knock at the door. My friend Nicole and our department secretary were both in tears when they informed me that our longtime colleague and star teacher, Roger Lundin, had suddenly and unexpectedly collapsed and died during the night. I have never experienced a deeper sense of dissonance than I did at that moment. My head acknowledged that it was true, but it felt wrong. I found it difficult to breathe. More tears, more numbness. Since it was still early in the morning, Nicole and I sat in my office together and tried to process. It was impossible. When students starting arriving, we all sat in the office suite together, praying. I don't think anyone met with their classes, unless it was just to be there for their students. Eventually I went home to go to sleep. I couldn't do anything else. Then I went to Brett's visitation and funeral. The following week I went to Roger's visitation and funeral. Honestly, I have no recollection at all of what I did in the week between.

Early onset winter again, this time much fiercer. Our department lost two of our most brilliant and beloved scholars and teachers, and I lost two friends. Our students were shell-shocked. To make matters worse, we were not close enough to the Thanksgiving holiday to call classes off. We had no choice but to muddle through the weeks together.

Although I had learned from my previous experience to give myself more grace and room to grieve, nothing ever prepares someone for something like this. I felt guilty about not telling these men how much they meant to me. I felt deep sorrow for their families. Brett was only forty-two years old, happily married with two teenaged children. He connected with others more easily than anyone I have ever met. Roger was a pillar in our department, a devoted teacher who knew everyone and seemed to remember everything. He had a loving wife who was looking forward to sharing retirement with her best friend. In short, our entire community was affected. I have always had difficulty dealing with the grief of others; when someone I love cries, I cry. Lots of tears were shed, and crying is exhausting.

In the subsequent weeks I felt so fortunate to have my friend Nicole in the department so that we could remind each other that this was an impossible situation. We needed to give each other explicit permission to let go of any expectations of ourselves to meet the goals we had originally set for either our personal lives or our work. You can't work when you are exhausted (Thing 4). You also can't fight off the desire to eat that piece of cheesecake or drink that glass of wine at the end of a long day of grief (Thing 9). Trying to do that, or feeling guilty when you can't, also saps your energy, and you sink further down.

Nicole is wise. She also happens to have written one of the most brilliant sentences that I have ever read. It is from her novel, *This Heavy Silence*. "Winter, like grieving, was a succession of false endings."[1] I thought of this sentence often during those days. I was grateful for the reminder that everyone in our community was going to be debilitated this way—in waves. We all had to learn how to give grace to ourselves and to our students and then to be prepared to do it again and again. Even the grammatical structure of this sentence contains a deep truth: you can't solve grief any more than you can prevent sorrowful events from happening to you. Winter sometimes lingers.

Are you struggling in an early onset winter right now? This, too, shall pass, but it will not leave without a trace. Those traces make us who we are.

CHUCK OUT CHUNK THINKING

It is only now, years later, that I see how low my energy had dipped that particular November. This happens when I am ill too. I quickly come to believe that the illness is my new reality and that I'm never going to feel well again. For me, the spiritual work I must do at this time is to ask God for perspective. Suffering, pain, and death are inevitable, but even these powerful things will not last forever.

I want to be transparent here: remembering this fact is one of the very hardest things for me to do. When I was pregnant, I started believing I would live the rest of my life with constant, low-level nausea. As I mentioned earlier, after I had an infant, I thought that I would never have the time or attention span to read a book again, not to mention write one. My husband has become very adept at spotting this Who Hash, calling it out, and making me laugh when I succumb to it yet again. We have come

---

[1] Nicole Mazzarella, *This Heavy Silence: A Novel* (Brewster, MA: Paraclete, 2006), 157.

to call it "chunk thinking," and we are both guilty of it in different ways at different times. It's the kind of thinking that insists that whatever struggle you are having in that moment is never going to go away. It's faithless, godless, hopeless. And it's debilitating. Time to chuck it out.

But how? I wish I had better advice to give on this score. One of the things that helps me is to read and write in my journal. I've kept a journal since I was in high school, and I'm up to twenty-two volumes now. It's inspiring to read back through a difficult time in my life so that I can remember what it felt like to struggle that way and then to see how God brought me through it. I've got many, many examples of deep frustrations that God clearly redeemed. For instance, I didn't get accepted to graduate school the first year I applied. I had no idea at the time that if you want to get a PhD in English, you weren't supposed to let on that you love literature. I felt humiliated and confused. I went through a period of severe vocational doubt. But when I finished graduate school six years later, the position I hold now was open. It would not have been open one year previous or one year later. That's God. The perspective I gained from remembering God's love for me in this way is immense. Another example: I was single until I was thirty-five, and I remember a number of faithless years where I wrestled with God about that. When he did put the right man in my life, I was in a much better place to be married than I was at any other time in my life. I could go on and on.

Reading journals is just one way to gain perspective. Even if you don't keep a journal, it is helpful to think about your life in terms of seasons. This works on a large scale where you think about your youth as a spring, midlife as a summer of growth, aging as a brilliant autumn, and winter as a natural, others-focused decline toward death. I have always been energized by thinking this way.

It is one of the main reasons for the design of the liturgical calendar. It is deeply biblical, as Ecclesiastes makes clear.

For everything there is a season, and a time for every matter under heaven:

a time to be born, and a time to die;
a time to plant, and a time to pluck up what is planted;
a time to kill, and a time to heal;
a time to break down, and a time to build up;
a time to weep, and a time to laugh;
a time to mourn, and a time to dance;
a time to throw away stones, and a time to gather
    stones together;
a time to embrace, and a time to refrain from embracing;
a time to seek, and a time to lose;
a time to keep, and a time to throw away;
a time to tear, and a time to sew;
a time to keep silence, and a time to speak;
a time to love, and a time to hate;
a time for war, and a time for peace. (Eccl 3:1-8)

While it is easy to gloss over these words that we have heard read and sung so many times, Americans in particular have not fully received the wisdom in them. We want eternal youth and a life without suffering. In God's wisdom, we were not designed that way. There is a time for youth, and a time for the grace that only the aged can possess. "The glory of youths is their strength, but the beauty of the aged is their gray hair" (Prov 20:29).

It is time to remember that gray hair is beautiful. It is, as Proverbs reminds us, "a crown of glory" (16:39). It was with an eye on these biblical truths that Henry David Thoreau wrote the essay "Autumnal Tints." If you are entering the late summer and early autumn of your own life (as I am), this essay is a treat. Early in it, he describes the oft-overlooked beauty of pokeweed:

> We love to see any redness in the vegetation of the temperate zone. It is the color of colors. This plant speaks to our blood. It asks a bright sun on it to make it show to best advantage, and it must be seen at this season of the year. On warm hillsides its stems are ripe by the twenty-third of August. At that date I walked through a beautiful grove of them, six or seven feet high, on the side of one of our cliffs, where they ripen early. Quite to the ground they were a deep brilliant purple with a bloom, contrasting with the still clear green leaves. It appears a rare triumph of Nature to have produced and perfected such a plant, as if this were enough for a summer. What a perfect maturity it arrives at! It is the emblem of a successful life concluded by a death not premature, which is an ornament to Nature. What if we were to mature as perfectly, root and branch, glowing in the midst of our decay, like the Poke! I confess that it excites me to behold them.[2]

Thoreau wrote this essay near the end of his life because he wanted to be grateful for it. It is all about perspective. He later discusses the dying of a tree's leaves as a gift of nourishment to the next generation. "They that soared so loftily, how contentedly they return to dust again, and are laid low, resigned to lie and decay at the foot of the tree, and afford nourishment to new generations of their kind, as well as to flutter on high!"[3] Thoreau believed that the natural world illustrates this confident contentment. We are the ones who refuse it.

Thinking of one's life in terms of seasons is essential to flourishing, especially for women. Faculty members who have young

---

[2]Henry David Thoreau, *Natural History Essays*, rev. ed. (Layton, UT: Gibbs Smith, 2011), 142.
[3]Henry David Thoreau, Bradford Torrey, and Franklin Benjamin Sanborn, *The Writings of Henry David Thoreau: Excursions and Poems* (Palala, 2018), 270.

children at home are in a very different season of life than those who are the same age without children. Those who are married to a full-time homeworker are in a different season from those who are not. I know too many women who beat themselves up because they strain against this reality, as if trying to deny it. When you have small children at home, regardless of whether your spouse works out of the home full time, your vitality is being poured into a more important place. You simply must have different expectations for your career. Full stop.

Why is this so hard for most of us to do? I admit that when I had all the stresses of caring for a small child, I did a very poor job of remembering that "this, too, shall pass." Older mothers said this to me, but I couldn't really hear it. Stress and sleeplessness made me deaf. As if trying to manage childcare is not hard enough, like many other families with children, I kept getting ill. Whatever germs Donovan got at school, he brought home to the whole family. Like Tantalus, I would finally barely recover from illness, only to have that gigantic rock roll over me again. It turns out I also had a chronic condition. Increasing every year from before my son's birth until he was six years old, I struggled with sinus infections. I was allergic to both families of dust mites (yes, there are families) and the entire state of Illinois. It got so bad that I was in bed with an infection every three or four weeks and on a constant cycle of antibiotics, which devastated my immune system. I missed Donovan's fifth birthday party because I was in bed. I started building flex days into my syllabus: days where I'd write "TBD," knowing that at some point I would get ill, lose my voice, and have to shift the schedule around. Missing class caused stress, and the stress further compromised my immune system. I know that many other parents of young children have experienced exactly this kind of hellacious loop. Dante's *Inferno* comes to mind.

My own story of this particular season in my life has a happy ending. I finally got some help from a very good ear, nose, and throat doctor who told me that she has often had patients whose sinus scans don't tell the whole story. She advised surgery. I took her advice and got the "sinus extravaganza" procedure. She told me afterward that she took a very large mess of stuff out of my sinuses. My life changed overnight. But some of the change was also that Donovan got older and stopped bringing every little germ home to his momma for a gift. He had also finally grown out of the constant vigilance stage that was particularly exhausting to me. So my advice for faculty members in the young-children-at-home season (particularly women) is simple. Do whatever it takes to remind yourself that it will not be like this forever. Because it really won't.

RIDE THE U

My writing group has a private Facebook page that we have dubbed "Ride the U." A few years ago I read an article in *The Atlantic* that reports on a growing body of research indicating that Americans are fairly happy when we are in our twenties, but as we get to the young-children-at-home stage, our happiness declines, and we hit a nadir. But when we pass through midlife, partly because our own expectations for happiness later in life are often low, we find that we are happier than we thought we would be. Happiness maps out on a U.[4]

This is not the case for third-world countries, by the way, which should cause Americans to reflect with humility on our immense privilege. Money can alleviate a tremendous amount of anxiety as one gets older, so if you have it, be grateful that you have it. Thing 6: Receive grace, but achieve gratitude.

---

[4]Cari Romm, "Where Age Equals Happiness," *The Atlantic*, November 6, 2014, www.the atlantic.com/health/archive/2014/11/where-age-equals-happiness/382434/.

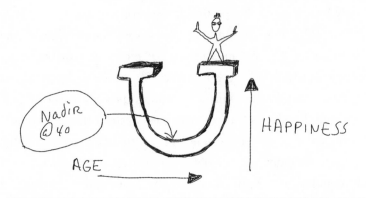

Figure 4.1. Ride the U

Since I'm seven to ten years older than everyone in my writing group, I take it as a solemn responsibility to remind them of the U. I often shout back to them from the upside. "Folks, it really is better up here!" If you don't have any friends who are riding the U in their fifties and sixties, then find some. There is joy here. Hopefully they will also remind you that there's no need worry about the lack of academic productivity when you are producing human beings. There's a season for that, and it's not now.

The reason why what Jonathan Rauch calls the "Happiness Curve" is so hard to see is that our culture does not have good narratives—like the one that Thoreau was trying to offer—about the transition from our forties into our fifties and beyond. We have only the language of crisis. But transition is not a crisis but an opportunity, so we need to learn to think about it differently. Rauch writes,

> Like adolescence, the happiness dip at midlife is developmen-
> tally predictable, and can be aggravated by isolation, confusion,
> and self-defeating thought patterns. Like adolescence, it can lead
> to crisis, but it is not, in and of itself, a crisis. Rather, like adoles-
> cence, it generally leads to a happier stage. In short, although

adolescence and the trough of the happiness curve are not at all the same biologically, emotionally, or socially, both transitions are commonplace and nonpathological. But one of them has a supportive social environment, whereas the other has . . . red sports cars.[5]

Riding the U should be a time for celebration, not crisis. There is no reason to settle for red sports cars when you can choose to enter a season of unparalleled productivity and joy. The wisdom we earn through suffering is the wisdom we have to give as we age. There is no substitute for experience, and our junior colleagues need us. They need us to model, with grace, the transition through middle age and beyond. Barbara Bradley Hagerty entered her own middle age with a desire to find the best models for managing that transition—how they live, what they do to handle it:

> Sometimes events in midlife, such as unemployment or illness, truly overwhelm a person, and the last thing I want to do is blame the victim. Still, reading through the stories and interviewing many of the writers, I realized that having a wider perspective, an investment in those you love, a willingness to be identified by your passions and not by your résumé, allow some people to unclench their hands and drop the burning coal that is a midlife crisis. The assaults of life can spiral you into an existential crisis. But they don't have to. You have a choice.[6]

Here in my early fifties, I'm just beginning this investigation myself. I long to be a model of grace, contentment, and joy to the younger educators in my circle of influence. I have a long way to go. Praise be to God that we never have to work out of our own

---

[5]Jonathan Rauch, "What Teenage Turmoil and Midlife Crises Have in Common," *The Atlantic*, April 22, 2018, www.theatlantic.com/magazine/archive/2018/05/jonathan-rauch -adolescence/556865/.
[6]Barbara Bradley Hagerty, *Life Reimagined: The Science, Art, and Opportunity of Midlife* (New York: Riverhead, 2017), 34.

strength. Since God made us all with different gifts, we should remember that flourishing will look a little different for each of us. But since an acorn was designed to grow into an oak, its glory is in being an oak in every season of its life. Not an elm, not a poplar—and certainly not some other kind of being altogether. What is required is the kind of poetic attention that helps us to delight in being who we are, created for this good work of teaching at this time in history. If we are inattentive, we will miss the show. Thoreau writes,

> But it requires a particular alertness, if not devotion to these phenomena, to appreciate the wide-spread, but late and un-expected glory of the Scarlet Oaks. . . . Most go in and shut their doors, thinking that bleak and colorless November has already come, when some of the most brilliant and memo-rable colors are not yet lit.
>
> This very perfect and vigorous one, about forty feet high, standing in an open pasture, which was quite glossy green on the twelfth, is now, the twenty-sixth, completely changed to bright dark scarlet,—every leaf, between you and the sun, as if it had been dipped into a scarlet dye. The whole tree is much like a heart in form, as well as color. Was not this worth waiting for? Little did you think, ten days ago, that that cold green tree would assume such color as this. Its leaves are still firmly attached, while those of other trees are falling around it. It seems to say,—"I am the last to blush, but I blush deeper than any of ye. I bring up the rear in my red coat. We Scarlet ones, alone of Oaks, have not given up the fight."[7]

We must choose to see the Scarlet Oak's luminous finish, not just its descent into winter's fallow. Was not this worth waiting for?

---

[7]Henry David Thoreau and Ralph Waldo Emerson, *Excursions* (New York: Crowell, 1913), 243.

FOR ADDITIONAL ENCOURAGEMENT

Cairns, Scott. *The End of Suffering: Finding Purpose in Pain.* Brewster, MA: Paraclete, 2009.

When we are suffering, we do not need a philosopher as much as we need a poet. Cairns is just the man for the job. I highly recommend the wisdom of this little book. I also recommend all of his poetry.

Rohr, Richard. *Falling Upward: A Spirituality for the Two Halves of Life.* San Francisco: Jossey-Bass, 2011.

Rohr, a Franciscan teacher, has been writing books for years that encourage us to be attentive to opportunities for spiritual growth. "A journey into the second half of our own lives awaits us all," he writes. "Not everybody gets there, even though all of us get older, and some of us get older than others" (vii).

Vaillant, George E. *Aging Well: Surprising Guideposts to a Happier Life from the Landmark Harvard Study of Adult Development.* New York: Little, Brown, 2003.

Vaillant's research created quite a stir when he first published it. The Harvard Study of Adult development followed 824 subjects from their teens into old age and asked them a lot of questions. I always find longitudinal research to be fascinating, and this is no exception. Meaningful engagement with others was on the list of factors that made for the happiest older people. If you are nearing retirement, it is useful to have a plan for staying connected in a rich and embodied way with others. Furthermore, if you enjoy longitudinal research, it is hard to beat the *Up* series of documentaries by Michael Apted. In 1964 Apted interviewed seven-year-old English schoolchildren, following up with them every seven years since. It is impossible not to be drawn in.

5 December

Christian Mindfulness

G rading, grading.
     Grading in the morning, grading in the noontime.
Grading, grading—
Grading till the sun goes down.

Am I singing your tune? Brothers and sisters, you are not alone. After more than twenty years of trying to negotiate the Christmas and end-of-semester craziness, I've got some good news and some bad news. The bad news is that December is December. At some level, this unhappy, annual collision of Advent with the end of the semester is something that just has to be endured. The good news is that there are strategies that can help. And the most important strategy can be exercised right now, right at this moment. Stop everything, close your eyes, and repeat after me: "This, too, shall pass." Trust me, it will. And here's some proof. It is December 19 as I'm writing these words. I submitted my grades yesterday, took my son out of school early to go to the latest *Star Wars* film, and am living the dream of real rest today. And yes, when I feel rested is when the urge to write comes on, but this only proves my point. You will become yourself again sooner than you think.

In short, in December—and really, in every month—the strategy behind all other strategies is mindfulness. Mindfulness is a trendy topic right now. It is used to describe anything from daily meditation techniques, to ways of eating, to new ways to approach thinking in general. There's lots of cognitive research that supports the importance of calming the mind by focusing exclusively on one's breathing. In this chapter, I want to talk about the importance of mindful decision making on a large scale and then about how practicing Christian mindfulness in the day-to-day zaniness of the Advent season can be a lifesaver for exhausted educators.

MINDFUL DECISIONS

Indulge me in telling you three true stories about large-scale decisions I have made — two of them were relatively easy, and one was really difficult.

Story number one. Back in the dark ages before the internet and social media, I used to send an annual Christmas letter. It was a hassle, but I also had fun putting it together. I enjoyed anticipating the letters I would receive from others in my wider circles of acquaintance. The tradition continued after I got married and beyond. I don't remember when I woke up and figured out that the stress involved in this annual activity was taking much more from me than it gave, especially when the semester was finishing up, grades were due, and Christmas was coming in spite of it all. My first flash of mindful recognition was: why not a summer letter instead? So I switched. But not long after that I had another flash of insight: why am I doing this at all? And that was that. I miss some things about it, but mostly it was an excellent decision to let it go.

Story number two. My mother is an incredible gardener. Every summer she battled the local deer to give us fresh tomatoes and cucumbers in our salads, and I grew an intense love for vegetables other people won't touch, like Swiss chard. When my husband and I moved into a house with a yard, we excitedly dug up the south side lawn and planted. For ten years we had delicious tomatoes, crisp cucumbers, and zucchini galore. We also had bugs, savage thistles from the pit of hell, and some kind of slug that ate squash roots that killed the plants overnight. Around here, if you want any kind of meaningful harvest, you need to plant by the second week of May. Teachers, however, are lucky to be counted among the walking dead in early May. Still I forced my husband to help me get out there and till that soil and buy the plants and get them in the ground. I forced myself, when "dog days" means dog-sized mosquitos, to go out and water, pick, and weed. I loved the output — truly there is nothing better than a garden tomato — and the planting satisfied my stewardship urges. But at one point the harsh reality set in. Why are we gardening if neither one of us actually enjoys it? Furthermore, we never get out in produce what we put in, in terms of effort and money. Last summer we finally tore out the garden and grew back the grass. I now garden tomatoes and cucumbers in a wonderful invention called an EarthBox. Manageable, and just as delicious.

Story number three: Since Steve and I were in our mid-thirties when we married, we knew that we needed to start almost right away if we were to have children. Our son, Donovan, was born less than two years later. He was a difficult baby right from the start. (Let me alleviate your anxiety based on the previous stories — this is not about me giving up on my baby like I gave up on my Christmas letter and garden.) We couldn't even take him to a restaurant in his carrier like I would see other families do. On television I'd see fathers with their infants sleeping in a BabyBjörn at the Cubs game and cry. There is no way my son could handle that: he'd be wide awake, crying, in sensory overload. We would later find out he is on the autism spectrum, which explained a lot of things but also left me overwhelmed with emotion. But even before we had that diagnosis, we had to decide whether we would try for another child, and we decided that we would. We lost one baby at about six weeks but were never able to get pregnant after that. Since we didn't want our son to be raised as an only child, we began to talk about adoption. We got serious about it, went to meetings, and prayed. Meanwhile, we worked our professorial jobs and cared for our young son. But I will never forget how one night we were sitting at our backyard fire pit in October, both exhausted as usual, and had one of the most monumental discussions in our married lives. I very quietly pointed out that we couldn't even make time to talk about this decision. Do we really have room to adopt? We wept together because we already knew the answer.

What these three stories combine to describe is that mindfulness begins with the courage to make big decisions about your values, priorities, and time—and stick to them without guilt or shame.

Anne-Marie Slaughter hit a substantial nerve in 2012 when she stepped out of the acceptable narrative for ambitious career women and wrote an *Atlantic* piece titled "Why Women Still Can't Have It All."[1] She had been teaching with her husband at Princeton University (already a demanding job) when Secretary of State Hillary Clinton invited her to lead her policy planning team. Slaughter suspected that this was her time to "lean in," and she took it. For two years she commuted to Washington, DC, leaving her two sons to be cared for by her husband. Eventually, leaning in started to look more lean than in. On Sunday nights her young son would beg her not to leave the next day, and her older son began to have behavioral issues. Slaughter is not arguing that her absence caused all of the problems with her older son, and certainly not that her

---

[1]Anne-Marie Slaughter, "Why Women Still Can't Have It All," *The Atlantic*, June 13, 2012, www.theatlantic.com/magazine/archive/2012/07/why-women-still-cant-have-it-all /309020/.

husband couldn't do an adequate job parenting. Instead, she learned something about herself that she did not expect: she wanted to be at home to help the family at this pivotal time in their lives. So she left Washington, returned to teach at Princeton, and wrote an article and a book that have reopened an old and important question for families everywhere.

Slaughter hit a nerve for a number of reasons, and I cannot address them all here. Her book *Unfinished Business* is worth reading because she hits on the principal reasons why most highly educated career women are put in a bind.[2] The problem is not having career ambitions, but working in institutions that value the bottom line over the health and well-being of their employees. It turns out that America is one of the worst countries in the world when it comes to valuing competition over care. Sometimes this comes down to explicit policies and practices that hurt women, such as inadequate maternity leave or inflexible meeting times. This is especially the case for lower-income workers, whose rigid policies hurt women twice.[3] But most of the time, especially for knowledge workers like us, the problem is the culture of the workplace. "Putting yourself forward is important at the right moment," argues Slaughter, "but so is pushing back against rules, structures, attitudes, and assumptions that still support a straight-on career path and stigmatize any worker who deviates from it, deferring promotions and bigger jobs to be able to spend time with loved ones. To see the whole picture, not just the shining role models at the top, but the employees, every bit as talented and motivated, who were pushed or shut out of leadership opportunities as their lives took unexpected detours."[4]

[2]Anne-Marie Slaughter, *Unfinished Business: Women Men Work Family* (New York: Random House, 2016).
[3]Slaughter, *Unfinished Business*, 64.
[4]Slaughter, *Unfinished Business*, 36.

She is suggesting that we push back against a productivity culture that does not understand grace.

When it comes to work and productivity, American culture is absurd. We often work on what Slaughter calls "Time Macho": I can work more hours than you, pull all-nighters, publish like a maniac, and so on. This is a deep-seated spiritual illness that very few prophets are willing to call out. The fact that our larger culture bows to the idol of productivity puts many of us Christian educators in a lose-lose scenario. Our Christian culture clearly values rest and family; our American work culture values productivity at the expense of everything.

The sad thing is that Christian colleges and schools often fare no better than secular ones. This is especially disgraceful because we should be leaders in putting our Christian values above the bottom line. We should have the best maternity leave policy, the most schedule flexibility, and the fewest time-wasting meetings. We should be known for giving grace while encouraging excellence. Instead, what I have observed at my own institution is that the American mentality, bolstered substantially by our patriarchal evangelical history, still seeps into the workplace in all kinds of insidious ways. It seeps into an administrator's comment that "this faculty is so entitled. I remember when faculty members would do things without expecting compensation for them." I've heard that comment said aloud. It seeps into letters written by male faculty members regarding a colleague in their own department who is up for promotion. "This person will need to write several more books before advancing." I read this exact comment when I was on faculty personnel committee. *Several* more books? At a liberal arts college that cherishes teaching? It seeps into the administrator who says, at a performance review, "Well, you've got one article here in a Christian scholarly journal, but . . ." This was said to me.

It seeps into our students, too, when they value grades and performance over learning. I've been saying *seep* when I should be
saying *flood*. I recently visited a cohort of our second-year faculty
members and several of them—all women—were in tears because
they felt so afraid of not being enough, not doing enough, to keep
their jobs. They weren't talking about advancement; they were
talking about survival.

I want to go on record to say that this is a serious problem, and
the problem is not that we have a lazy faculty. The problem is fear.
Faculty members are afraid because the institution is afraid. We are
afraid of not looking like the big boys. We are afraid of losing students. We are afraid of the eroding bottom line that plagues all institutions of higher education. When these fears run rampant, they
destroy much more than faculty morale. The twisted irony is that the
more we push faculty to work out of fear, the less we actually produce.

Many of us went into teaching precisely because we expected it
not to be a cutthroat career. Most of us wanted autonomy in the
classroom and flexibility in our schedules, especially during the
summer. I cannot pretend to know what I would have done if I was
working as a lawyer and not a professor, or if my husband was. But
I do know that my husband and I were among the fortunate ones
who could, at least for a time and not without losses, each both keep
our careers and raise our son. I had the benefit of a female department chair who was herself a mother. She went out of her way
to give the mothers in the department their first choice for the sched-
uling of classes. I know very well that with a different chair, those
first six years of my son's life would have been almost impossible for
me. I scheduled all my classes on Mondays, Wednesdays, and
Fridays; my husband scheduled all of his on Tuesdays and Thursdays.
He did what I could never do: he left at 4:30 a.m. for a college one
hour away and taught four long classes, one after another. We were

completely exhausted. It was the hardest time in our lives. But in spite of all this stress, we never succumbed to the temptation of thinking that we were trying to "have it all." I worked because I love my job, and because I also knew from day one that I would be a better mother if I spent some time working at something that was not mothering. Steve was not predisposed to leave his job to be a stay-at-home dad, though he could have done that. Additionally, I never expected him to offer his support that way, though I would not have been overly surprised if he did. I know some women who are the primary breadwinners for their family, and they will be the first to tell you that this comes with its own set of joys and challenges, both for the working wives and the husbands.

One of my friends who has a working spouse and three children hates the term *work-life balance*. "There is no such thing," she insists. And she is right. Gary Keller also puts it very simply: "A balanced life is a lie."[5] I'm raising these issues in a chapter on mindfulness to encourage readers that it is not about balance but priorities. The only way to survive the hard decisions every family has to make is to be mindful about those decisions and then to accept the consequences. The very simple truth is that if you work at a place that does not allow you flexible hours, your decisions will look different from mine. If you want to raise a family, you have to make harder decisions: Who will stay home, and how often? Which caregivers will we choose? Should I look for a different job?

Don't get me wrong: I am 100 percent in favor of the attitude shifts that Slaughter and others are fighting for. America has deeply systemic idolatry issues that make it difficult for people to be whole. One of my closest friends is the wife of an executive at a major Hollywood studio and the mother of three sons. His all-consuming

---

[5]Gary Keller and Jay Papasan, *The ONE Thing: The Surprisingly Simple Truth Behind Extraordinary Results* (Austin: Bard, 2013), 73.

career not only prevents her from pursuing a career of her own, but it also regularly strains their marriage. The problem here is not my friends. The problem is the immoderate expectations placed on him by the workaholic culture of the film industry. My friends can't change the expectations at his workplace (at least not without a pyrrhic fight), so they must be mindful enough to return to their decisions *as decisions they made*. He could work elsewhere, but they both know that this work is his passion. He needs regular reminders of her sacrifice, and she needs real breaks from the drudgery of driving her boys all over Los Angeles. Without mindfulness of the decisions they have made and the seasonal consequences of those decisions, the whole thing will fall apart.

My point is that everyone's situation is different, and there are no easy answers to be found anywhere. When my husband and I made the difficult decision regarding adoption, I found great comfort in reminding myself that every family looks different. We do well not to live by some ghostly standard most women (and many men) carry around in our heads of what a good family should look like: a lovely house within walking distance from work and church, 2.5 smiling children, and an uninterrupted career trajectory. These are unreasonable expectations, and it is the expectations that make us miserable. When I began to mindfully consider the fact that my family is the one that God gave me to have right now, my attitude began to change. I could grieve the fact that I have only one child and then move on to embrace what having only one child enables me to do. If you have three children, rejoice, but don't expect to be able to get as much done as someone who doesn't—and that's perfectly okay. Furthermore, let's all take a big step back and look around. It is easy for married folks to forget that our single friends, particularly women, have had to make the same decision to embrace the life that God has given them. For most of them it is even harder to do because their grief has gone completely unnoticed. Think about that for a while, and don't complain when your promotion is delayed because you opted to put off writing that book.

Mindfulness in this larger sense means either coming to terms with the choices that we have made or having the courage to make different ones. As I mentioned in my last chapter, a very wide-angled outside perspective is critical here. That perspective must come with deliberately asking this question: Is what I am doing now the best thing *for me* to be doing? I mean this question in big ways and small ways. And necessarily personal ways. This cannot be one size fits all. After contemplating this question, if you choose to set aside or delay your career in order to be with your children, you have made the right choice. They are with us for so short a period of time, and though they might delay your tenure, who cares? Does God care when you get promoted to full professor — or if you do at all? The key is to accept this with joy. If you and your spouse each choose to continue your careers and raise a family, you must accept with joy that this means a slower advancement trajectory, trading off with your spouse, or other compromises. The lie at the center of "having it all" is entitlement. Who is entitled to it all? No one. If you are teaching in the United States of America, you more than likely have enough resources to live above the poverty line, raise reasonably sane children, and enjoy your life. I'll never forget the way I felt at breakfast when BAJ and I looked at each other, weary from our many responsibilities, and acknowledged the truth: this *is* thriving! We chose this! This is what we signed up for. There are many, many people in this country and in the world who would give anything to have our career and our families.

If you find that you cannot do this job and raise a family the way you want to, then this means you need to take a hard look at what you are willing and able to change. Has there been anything wiser than the famous Serenity Prayer, attributed to Reinhold Niebuhr?

God, grant me the serenity to accept the things I
    cannot change,
Courage to change the things I can,
And wisdom to know the difference.

There's a reason why it's called the serenity prayer. Mindfulness is the key to serenity.

MINDFUL DAYS

The Advent season is the perfect time to begin practicing mindfulness in our day-to-day lives, which is also the best way to get through the winter. When things get busy like they always do at the end of the semester and before Christmas, the days fly by. We begin to feel like our lives are living us and not the other way around. One of the great things about the mindfulness industry is that the promoters all share one thing: the belief that all we ever have is the moment right in front of us. The greatest freedom of all is the freedom we have to determine what to do with this moment.

Mindfulness is associated with Buddhist practices, but Buddhism has no corner on meditation. What Buddhism has often done better than Christianity is remembering the importance of *practice*. It turns out that none of this comes to us naturally. We've got to work at learning how to be mindful, how to live fully in the present moment. I have found the Ignatian spiritual exercises to be a great bridge to learning this kind of mindfulness. One of the cornerstones of the practice is the daily examen. At the end of the day — but also, at any point during the day — we ask some version of the questions "where did I most sense the presence of God today?" and "where did I least sense the presence of God today?"

The point is that the repeated practice will eventually reveal that mindfulness is the key to sensing God's presence in all parts of the day. It takes mindfulness to obey Colossians 3:15: "let the peace of Christ rule in your hearts, to which indeed you were called in the one body. And be thankful." We have a choice to live in thankfulness, to be present to the beauty of the gift of each moment of each day. It is a choice that we can only learn by practice.

As with any practice, you've got to clear time to do it, and it works even more powerfully when you make it a habit. There are several apps that help with that. The one that I rely on is *Calm*. *Calm* has a collection of wonderful sleep stories that I listen to almost every night. Another one I know of is *Headspace*. There are others. Both of these services are fee-based and provide a series of guided meditations for a variety of situations. They help you to focus on your breathing and learn how to simply be present to yourself without judgment.

One of my favorite Christian resources for thinking about this is Martin Laird's *Into the Silent Land: A Guide to the Christian Practice of Contemplation.*[6] I learned from Laird the practice of choosing a prayer word to help guide me as I enter prayer. The goal is to empty your mind of everything and just breathe in and breathe out that word. I'm a big believer in choosing a word of the year for each year, and there's no reason why that word couldn't be the same as your prayer word. Last year I chose *peace*. One year I had *simplify*, and another *joy*. Sit for a while in prayer until your biggest need comes to you, and then just breathe it in and out until your soul resets.

Laird also does a fine job of reminding us how important and underrated silence is in our culture. All introverts already know

---

[6]Martin Laird, *Into the Silent Land: A Guide to the Christian Practice of Contemplation* (Oxford: Oxford University Press, 2006).

this, but it is vital for our extroverted friends too. The fact is that all Christians need space and quiet to "be still and know that I am God" (Ps 46:10). Without the stillness and the quiet, there is no knowing. There is no chance for that small, still voice to speak.

I know very well that I am preaching to the choir here and that most of you will say, "But that's exactly the problem. How do I get that space, that silence?" And that's the rub. We have to be creative and willing to make some sacrifices. You might have to have that painful conversation with your husband when you explain that you really will explode if you don't get some time alone, especially before the Christmas craziness starts. My husband knows that I am much more myself when I'm able to be alone in the house. So we have a standing agreement for him to leave the house to me on Tuesdays. Here again, this works now because our son is in school. If your children are at home, you have to decide how much you are willing to pay to get some time where you can be alone. If you are able to pay a babysitter and go out occasionally, you can also pay a babysitter to give you a few hours off on a regular basis. This is just for a season of your life, and you need to remember that refilling your energy tank is worth it. If you cannot ever find any time to be alone, then it is time to go back to the larger questions I asked above. Is what I am doing now what I really should and want to be doing? If the answer is no, you need to set aside time for creativity and pray for courage to change something.

I want to end this section by arguing that I think the virtues of doing absolutely nothing are underrated. I have friends who think that they need to say yes to every social or work opportunity and then don't understand why they are exhausted. This goes back to what I was talking about in chapter two. We have got to know ourselves, how much sleep we need, and how much alone time we need. I personally need a whole lot of afternoons of doing absolutely nothing at Christmas and in the summer so that I can go back to doing a lot of work all day long in the school year. I am a better person when I do.

MINDFUL DECEMBER

Advent is the ideal season to practice both mindful decisions and mindful days because the need is so great, and the occasion is perfect. Advent is meant to be a season of reflective and hopeful waiting. It is meant to focus us in expectation of the Christ child, the greatest gift given to humankind. You can't be full of hopeful expectation if you are running around like a crazy person, barely getting your grades in and then rushing off to the store for last-minute gifts. How can this December be different? Is it possible to have a mindful December instead of a mindless one?

Our church has often offered an Advent retreat. At first it seemed impossible for me to take an entire weekend in early December to focus on waiting for the Lord, but it soon became impossible for me not to do it. It was during one of these retreats that I first learned the ancient practice of *lectio divina* (divine reading) and had the idea to bring the practice into my classes (as I explain in chapter 12). One year we were instructed to meditate on Luke's account of Jesus's presentation at the temple:

> Now there was a man in Jerusalem whose name was Simeon; this man was righteous and devout, looking forward to the consolation of Israel, and the Holy Spirit rested on him. It had been revealed to him by the Holy Spirit that he would not see death before he had seen the Lord's Messiah. Guided by the Spirit, Simeon came into the temple; and when the parents brought in the child Jesus, to do for him what was customary under the law, Simeon took him in his arms and praised God, saying,

"Master, now you are dismissing your servant in peace,
    according to your word;
for my eyes have seen your salvation,
    which you have prepared in the presence of all peoples,
a light for revelation to the Gentiles
    and for glory to your people Israel."

And the child's father and mother were amazed at what was being said about him. Then Simeon blessed them and said to his mother Mary, "This child is destined for the falling and the rising of many in Israel, and to be a sign that will be opposed so that the inner thoughts of many will be revealed — and a sword will pierce your own soul too." (Lk 2:25-35)

This exercise encourages us to enter into Simeon's emotional response to finally seeing the promised Christ child. When we think deeply about how long Simeon might have been actively "looking forward to the consolation of Israel," we can enter into the work of hopeful expectation ourselves. We learn how mindfulness can grow our faith in God's promises to the Church and to us.

Starting the month with some sort of advent retreat is an ideal way to regain the perspective that educators especially need during this challenging time. I have similarly found that creating enough space to have a mindful December requires some advanced planning. Bearing in mind that my husband has accurately dubbed our family the "last-minute Lakes," it is also true that the times we have planned ahead for the holidays were infinitely better than the ones when it suddenly occurred to us in November that we needed to make holiday plans. Many families I know have a schedule for the holidays in which they work out all the complicated trade-offs in advance. This kind of planning is essential for all educators.

What is even more necessary is the ability to set healthy boundaries and keep them without shame. I have not always been popular in my extended family because of my holiday boundaries. Since I always have to teach on the Monday after Thanksgiving, driving someplace far away with a screaming baby in the backseat is not going to give me the Thanksgiving break that will make me feel even remotely thankful. But Christmas break in Florida? I'm in — as long as you don't mind me collapsing by your swimming pool. Since my work rises to an insane level of intensity right at the time that everyone else is baking cookies, I'm just not going to be doing the cooking. Sorry. Not this year, and probably not any year. I will be available to help as long as I don't have to make decisions about anything. If we are gathering at my house and I am responsible for the cooking, it will be a nice and easy turkey breast in the slow cooker, roasted sweet potatoes, garlicky green beans, and the best wine I can afford. I used to get angry both as a high school teacher and in my early years of being a professor when people mentioned how much time I got "off." I sometimes want to be snarky — "How many books do *you* write on your time 'off'?" — but I know it doesn't help. The fact is that we work in a profession that most people will never understand. We can keep the crazy to ourselves, but if we do, we need to set boundaries.

There is decidedly no "one size fits all" when it comes to the boundary setting necessary for a joyful and mindful December. If doing the holiday cooking and baking gives you joy, then do it! If you hate it, then you need to find a way to alter the plans long enough in advance for others to acknowledge the sanity boundary you just established. Either way, I strongly encourage you to sit down before things get busy and think about ways you can protect some precious time to restore yourself after a busy semester. For example, do you really need to attend every single Christmas gathering to which you are invited? Is there a gift-trading system you can suggest to keep your extended family's gift-giving from spiraling out of control? Does your department need to hold that evening Christmas party with the white elephant disaster nobody really likes?

If you want to have more energy for Christmasy things at Christmas, there are also plenty of things you can try to make the end of the semester much easier. Try a graded class discussion (see chapter nine). If possible, do not assign end-of-term papers. The last thing you need to do before Christmas break is sit behind a stack of research essays. It turns out that the students don't want to write them either. Choose your pain. Try some of the paper-grading strategies I mention in chapter eight.

When it comes to the unavoidable end-of-term grading—like exams—you simply have to find out what works best for you. I've tried it multiple ways, but for me pushing through it as quickly as possible is best. I try to grade immediately after the exams come in, and then for a focused time very early in the mornings until the work is finished. This year I had only two senior seminar papers left to assess when I headed over to the home of one of my friends who was holding a grading party in his house. What a treat—he had hot buttered rum, snacks, and a bowlful of phrases that he challenged us to use in our feedback to the students. This year, my phrase was from Watto in *The Phantom Menace*: "Mind tricks don't work on me." I knew I wouldn't be able to concentrate much around my friends, but I wanted to be with the misery-loving company. I also wanted to leave early and victorious. The victorious part I kept to myself: don't ever announce that you have turned in your grades to a group of bedraggled colleagues!

Finally, set up a meaningful reward system and use it. Teaching is hard enough, but grading is a whole other stocking full of coal.

As I will discuss later, most grading at the college level (assessing essays) is making one big decision after another, with the added psychological trauma of knowing that your decisions won't always be appreciated at the other end. So reward yourself. Set up power hours of grading punctuated by a walk to Starbucks for something you wouldn't normally indulge in. Grade hard in the morning, and then go to the movies by yourself in the afternoon while your children are still in school. Set up something indulgent that you know will relax you: a trip to the spa for a massage or— my favorite—a salt float. There is nothing that says, "You made it!" like floating inside of a completely dark, warm, and quiet pod for an hour with absolutely no sensory stimulation. Euphoria.

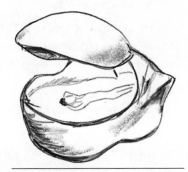

Figure 5.1. Salt float

Whether you are a high school or college teacher, a little creativity and advanced planning can go a long way into easing the end-of-the-semester crazy. You owe it to yourself and your family to be able to enter into the silence of Christmas with hope in your heart. This *is* thriving, and you should be able to relish every minute of it.

FOR ADDITIONAL ENCOURAGEMENT

Brown, Brené. *Daring Greatly: How the Courage to Be Vulnerable Transforms the Way We Live, Love, Parent, and Lead.* New York: Avery, 2015.

When you make big decisions about how to parent, shame can come knocking at the door pretty quickly. Career women in particular have to deal with a Christian culture that still does not understand us very well.

Brené Brown is a shame researcher whose work became an overnight sensation. This book is one of many. It, along with her famous TED talks, teach readers how to be more resilient to shame. She also has some excellent insight into how to parent children without shaming them.

Clarkson, Sally, and Nathan Clarkson. *Different: The Story of an Outside-the-Box Kid and the Mom Who Loved Him.* Carol Stream, IL: Tyndale House, 2017.

This book brought healing tears to my eyes. It serves as a reminder that God made every family and every person unique. The question is always: Can I receive this gift with joy and entrust it all to God?

Laird, Martin. *Into the Silent Land: A Guide to the Christian Practice of Contemplation.* Oxford: Oxford University Press, 2006.

If you get the opportunity to go on a silent Advent retreat with your church, take it, and bring along this book. It will remind you that Christians, of all people, should know how to live in mindful appreciation for this moment, the only moment that we have.

Pieper, Josef, and James V. Schall. *Leisure: The Basis of Culture.* San Francisco: Ignatius, 2009.

This is one of my favorite books. Pieper makes explicit the link between the idol of productivity and spiritual lethargy. In short, if you mindlessly work all the time, you will have nothing left to do but amuse yourself to death. This is the American way, and it is a disaster. If you haven't read it, create more leisure time so you can.

Slaughter, Anne-Marie. *Unfinished Business: Women Men Work Family.* New York: Random House, 2016.

As I mentioned above, this book is a solid read for knowledge professionals who are trying to be responsible parents.

January

Build a Soul Shelf

As a dedicated and voracious reader, I've always been fascinated by what people choose to read. Given the busyness of our culture and its assault on our leisure time, I'm even more fascinated by what people choose to reread. Why would anyone spend time in a text they've already digested? I once met a man at a conference who told me that he read the entire *Lord of the Rings* trilogy every year. He had been doing this ritual for at least ten years and had not wearied of the practice at all.

Most intellectuals return to certain texts, but have any of us ever stopped to wonder why we do? More than ten years ago, I did. It was January, and I was rereading Annie Dillard's *Pilgrim at Tinker Creek*, a book that I have always loved. Reading it caused me to have a poetic outburst in my journal. Here's what I wrote:

> I'm breathless, stunned again from reading Annie Dillard, thinking how beautiful this writing is, wondering why I spend time reading any other sorts of things, wondering at how those other things seeping into my soul have degraded it. How many times do I need to read Jack Kerouac before it drops me into a sack of *nearly* beautiful gems, but it is a sack from which I cannot escape? There is no air in there. In Dillard, there is

closeness, it is not all breezy, but there is something to hold like Julian of Norwich held a hazelnut in the palm of her hand and saw that all shall be well. All is made by God. The purpose of the artist is to burn in that glory, to light it as one does a wick, for everyone else to see. She herself goes to the flames, extinguished, burnt into the poems. It *is* a romantic vision, but oh so beautiful. The artist is she who has nothing but possesses everything, such as Emerson, Thoreau, and Dillard have said. The contemplative, they who teach the *vita contempletiva.* Light the way; wake us up.

I have deliberately not edited my own embarrassingly effusive prose to make a point. Reading something beautiful stirred my soul and made me long to come out of myself into a different kind of life. It made me crave a life surrounded by beauty, simplicity, and love. It made me wonder if I was ritually exposing myself to the wrong things. And it made me desire more of the sensibility that Annie Dillard gave me, the sudden awareness of the whole world as the beautiful gift it is.

I'm convinced that only the arts can stir the soul like this. It is the work of what *Christianity Today* has called "beautiful orthodoxy." I'm also convinced that when we return to the things that give us glimpses of beauty, those glimpses are strong enough to make us feel that we are nearer to the glory of God. The bizarrely sudden and grace-filled surge of this feeling is described by C. S. Lewis in *Surprised by Joy* and *The Pilgrim's Regress.* Lewis does a great service by clearly separating this feeling from happiness. Happiness comes from the root *hap*, from which we get "happenstance." Happiness is thus dependent on circumstances that make us happy: the weather today is nice; I just got a promotion; I'm heading to breakfast with a good friend; and so on. But joy is something deeper. It is a condition of the soul when it recognizes along with Julian that "all things are well, all manner of things are well."[1] As with happiness, there is an accidental quality to its surfacing in our lives. It cannot be produced at will. But the conditions for experiencing it are nonetheless all around us, all the time. A surge of joy can come out of a deep blue sky simply because it is blue. The problem is we don't see it.

But the good news for us is that poets understand this ephemeral quality of joy very well. When I was an undergraduate, I intently studied the poetry of Wallace Stevens, even writing a hundred-page senior thesis on the imagistic beauty of his poetry. I was deep in the darkest bowels of the library reading his journals and letters when I came across a sentence I will never forget. Stevens had been on one of his customary long walks, and he later wrote, "God, what a thing blue is!" I don't remember what came before or after that, but this one line has stayed with me. This is the joy that motivates poetry. This is the joy we can get from reading it, too, if we are willing to be patient.

It is because of my longing to be surprised by joy that I created my soul shelf. There is one bookcase in my bedroom (and a metaphorical one too) in which I keep all the books and other materials that nudge me to the kind of receptivity that led Stevens to proclaim his love for the color blue. It is where I turn during those inevitably bleak January, February, and March days when my soul feels dead. As you will see in chapter ten, I don't agree with much that A. G. Sertillanges says about how intellectuals should read, but he's spot on when he reminds us that in times of spiritual or intellectual depression, "each one should watch himself, note what helps him, keep at hand together his remedies for the sicknesses of the soul and not hesitate to go back and back to the same cordial

---

[1]Julian of Norwich, *The Complete Julian of Norwich* (Brewster, MA: Paraclete Press, 2009).

or the same antidote until these have utterly lost their efficacy."[2] Educators need a soul shelf.

Of course, the kinds of things that will end up on your soul shelf will be different from mine. But I doubt that either one of us will have anything that is merely sentimental. Sentimentalism is too cheaply gained an emotion, and repeated exposure to it has a soul-deadening effect. It offers only temporary escape. Our souls eventually reject it, like an organ transplant that seemed to go well at first but in the end became poison to the body. I've come to distrust any writer who has a false or otherworldly imagination that wants to leave this one behind. Instead, a writer's imagination

Figure 6.1. Soul shelf

should be bent on showing us how to see this world for the God-given beauty it has — and should never be afraid to show how the fall has impacted it. One of the best articulations of the kind of imaginative writing I'm talking about can be seen in Robert Frost's "Birches."

> When I see birches bend to left and right
> Across the lines of straighter darker trees,
> I like to think some boy's been swinging them.
> But swinging doesn't bend them down to stay
> As ice-storms do. Often you must have seen them
> Loaded with ice a sunny winter morning
> After a rain. They click upon themselves
> As the breeze rises, and turn many-colored

---

[2]Sertillanges, A. G., OP, and James V. Schall, SJ, *The Intellectual Life: Its Spirit, Conditions, Methods*, trans. Mary Ryan (Washington, DC: The Catholic University of America Press, 1992), 155.

As the stir cracks and crazes their enamel.
Soon the sun's warmth makes them shed crystal shells
Shattering and avalanching on the snow-crust—
Such heaps of broken glass to sweep away
You'd think the inner dome of heaven had fallen.
They are dragged to the withered bracken by the load,
And they seem not to break; though once they are bowed
So low for long, they never right themselves:
You may see their trunks arching in the woods
Years afterwards, trailing their leaves on the ground
Like girls on hands and knees that throw their hair
Before them over their heads to dry in the sun.
But I was going to say when Truth broke in
With all her matter-of-fact about the ice-storm
I should prefer to have some boy bend them
As he went out and in to fetch the cows—
Some boy too far from town to learn baseball,
Whose only play was what he found himself,
Summer or winter, and could play alone.
One by one he subdued his father's trees
By riding them down over and over again
Until he took the stiffness out of them,
And not one but hung limp, not one was left
For him to conquer. He learned all there was
To learn about not launching out too soon
And so not carrying the tree away
Clear to the ground. He always kept his poise
To the top branches, climbing carefully
With the same pains you use to fill a cup
Up to the brim, and even above the brim.
Then he flung outward, feet first, with a swish,

Kicking his way down through the air to the ground.
So was I once myself a swinger of birches.
And so I dream of going back to be.
It's when I'm weary of considerations,
And life is too much like a pathless wood
Where your face burns and tickles with the cobwebs
Broken across it, and one eye is weeping
From a twig's having lashed across it open.
I'd like to get away from earth awhile
And then come back to it and begin over.
May no fate willfully misunderstand me
And half grant what I wish and snatch me away
Not to return. Earth's the right place for love:
I don't know where it's likely to go better.
I'd like to go by climbing a birch tree,
And climb black branches up a snow-white trunk
Toward heaven, till the tree could bear no more,
But dipped its top and set me down again.
That would be good both going and coming back.
One could do worse than be a swinger of birches.

The poem's gathering metaphor is the poet as a young boy, a "swinger of birches." The speaker imagines the movement between earth and heaven, between the matter-of-factness of this world and the eternal truths it touches, as the movement of a boy leaping out away from the tree and swinging down on the branches. Notice that the speaker longs to be a swinger of birches exactly when "life is too much like a pathless wood" and "one eye is weeping / From a twig's having lashed across it open." The speaker would like to get away from these difficulties, but he does not succeed in finding joy by the leap alone, as if the goal was to escape into the heavens.

The speaker succeeds instead by learning to enjoy the movement between heaven and earth by way of the only tools available to us on earth. "May no fate willfully misunderstand me / And half grant what I wish and snatch me away / Not to return. Earth's the right place for love: / I don't know where it's likely to go better." Earth's the right place for love because if our love is only other-worldly, it does us no good at all. Instead, the speaker would like to get away and come back by being a swinger of birches, to climb "*toward* heaven, till the tree could bear no more" and dipped its top to set him back down again, filled with the joy and energy of his flight. That, dear reader, is a picture of what the best creative work does for us. It gives us a glimpse of the really real and sets us back down gently to take the vision into the day-to-day, grown-up world that we inhabit.

This January I encourage you to investigate, collect, and return to the works of art that give you a surge of the child-like joy of swinging on birch trees. The things that inspire me the most generally fit into categories not of fiction and nonfiction, nor of poetry and film, but of "beauty," "simplicity," and "love." My division is somewhat arbitrary, of course, because many of the items could be catalogued in all three groups. All of them lead to joy. I wanted to keep things simple to help inspire your own collection of items that stir your soul and encourage you to carry on.

BEAUTY

In his book *The Experience of God*, David Bentley Hart names three experiences that he thinks point to the existence of God: being, consciousness, and bliss.[3] *Bliss* is the name he gives to the way we feel when we experience beauty. It is somewhat synonymous with

---

[3]David Bentley Hart, *The Experience of God: Being, Consciousness, Bliss* (New Haven: Yale University Press, 2014).

the way I've used the term *joy* above. *Beauty* has been a contested term for a long time, and I won't bore you with the particularities of that debate. But I think people know by instinct that beauty is not something thin—like prettiness or sentimentality—but something solid, rich, and necessary to remind us how desirable the abundant life we have in Christ truly is.

When I first started teaching college students, God did a tremendous work in me regarding this idea of desire and how it connects to beauty. As an idealistic young intellectual, I was striving for perfection and control over my own life, even my spiritual life, and had very little understanding of grace. I could have told you what it meant, of course, and that we were all recipients of it, but I was far from comprehending it. What I had yet to learn was that there were certain things that had become idols in my life precisely because my desire for them was out of whack. I remember the shock of recognition when I read that idolatry was excessive desire for something that is not God. If we have idols, it is because we have misnamed the true object of our desire, which is God. We think we want one thing—the perfect spouse, the perfect job, the perfect home, whatever it is—but what we really want is God.

There is no way to effect in yourself the kind of radical reorientation that I'm talking about, though many writers have tried to invite us into it. Notably, Dallas Willard talks about the misplaced efforts of sin management. I have often taught this idea to my students by using the example of pornography. If you are trying to manage the sin of pornography by an effort of your will—by mortifying the flesh, to use a Puritan expression—you will never succeed. The idol is still in play, and you are asking the wrong question. Instead, if you ask how to fix your eyes on Jesus so that all other desires line up with his, you are on a better path. I remember when it occurred to me that the one thing I needed in my spiritual life was to recognize that Jesus was what I actually wanted. Jesus said that "the kingdom of heaven is like a merchant in search of fine pearls; on finding one pearl of great value, he went and sold all that he had and bought it" (Mt 13:45-46). It was as if I had been deaf in one ear, and the deafness cleared: *finding the kingdom of heaven means learning how to locate the pearl and treasure it.* I had been going for the oyster and missed the pearl. I also finally understood that beauty is anything that reveals the pearl to be the pearl that it is. This is nothing new, of course. Augustine wrote about it all the time. When you look at something beautiful, it should draw your heart up to the giver of that beautiful thing and melt you into praise. And what you have been given, and are given every moment of every day, is unbelievable amounts of grace.

Who wouldn't want to surround themselves with things that remind you of the true object of your soul's desire? There is nothing gnostic here, because it starts with the fact of your birth and spirals into every conceivable direction: sunlight in the leaves of the tree outside your window; the warm, fragrant cup of coffee in your hand. To begin the beauty section of your soul shelf, ask the question, "What makes me remember that my life here is a gift of immeasurable beauty?" And you might add, "What am I reading, watching, or listening to when I do experience that kind of bliss?" Here are some of the things that I do that work for me.

Bach, J. S. Cello concertos.

Musical education is a real weakness in my own intellectual formation, but not in my spiritual life. I know what stirs me even if I cannot explain why. I've never been able to hear the first three notes of the prelude of the Cello Suite No. 1 in G without tears coming to my eyes. Mischa Maisky's performance of it on YouTube had over 36 million views the last time I checked. This is such an antidote for my own intellectual ills that I must work very hard not to overuse it.

Dillard, Annie. *Pilgrim at Tinker Creek*. New York: Harper, 2013.

This book, as well as pretty much everything else by Dillard, will move you to appreciate the power of words and the beauty of the natural world. She's the Christian female Thoreau that my soul was longing for before I finally found her.

Levertov, Denise. *The Stream and the Sapphire: Selected Poems on Religious Themes*. New York: New Directions, 1997.

This collection of poems, taken from several volumes of Levertov's poetry, carries on in the spirit of Julian of Norwich and is never far from my side. The scholar-poet and my former dean, Jill Baumgaertner, told me that she also keeps this collection on her bedside table. Levertov writes poems about the grace of God that make you recognize its depth in ways you never considered before. She even has several remarkable poems about Julian's visions. I'd be remiss to not put this collection at the top of my list.

Robinson, Marilynne. *Gilead*. New York: Farrar, Straus and Giroux, 2004.

Even though I've written quite a bit about this insightful novel, I still love it. It is followed by two equally poetic others in a series, *Home* and *Lila*. In the first, Robinson helps us to see the world through the eyes of a faithful minister nearing the end of his life. All three retell the parable of the prodigal son in a way that helps us to see why it is so important to learn how to become more and more like the father.

The Showings of Julian of Norwich.

There are different editions of this English text written by the medieval anchorite Julian. Her visions were full of the understanding that this world is a beautiful gift that God holds in the palm of his hand. "All things shall be well, and all manner of things shall be well." What's a soul shelf without this book?

Undset, Sigrid, and Brad Leithauser. *Kristin Lavransdatter*. Edited and translated by Tiina Nunnally. New York: Penguin Classics, 2005.

Undset, a twentieth-century Norwegian writer, won the Nobel prize in literature largely because of this trilogy of novels. I love them intensely. They tell the story of a medieval Norwegian young woman who has to learn how to navigate the tension between her passions and her responsibilities. Make sure you read the Tiina Nunnally translation.

Wiman, Christian, ed. *Joy: 100 Poems.* New Haven: Yale University Press, 2017.

A former student and friend gave me this wonderful book. As soon as I read the introduction, it became a part of my soul shelf. Wiman, a brilliant poet, introduces this collection in such a stirring way that it will make you wonder why you haven't made more time in your life for poetry. He explains that "if you are trying to understand why a moment of joy can blast you right out of the life to which it makes you all the more lovingly and tenaciously attached, or why this lift into pure bliss might also entail a steep drop of concomitant loss, or how in the midst of great grief some fugitive and inexplicable joy might, like one tiny flower in a land of ash, bloom — well, in these cases the dictionary is useless."[4] What we need is poetry. If poetry scares you, it is time to get over it. This is an excellent place to start.

SIMPLICITY

I receive tremendous joy and rejuvenation from the pursuit of simplicity. Since we work so much with our minds, it is particularly important to have our desks cleared and our lives in order as much as possible. While reading *Walden* as an undergraduate I found that my soul resonated with Thoreau's on this point: having more stuff, including more stuff to do, does not give us joy, and often robs us of it. "Our life is frittered away by detail," he writes. "An honest man has hardly need to count more than his ten fingers, or in extreme cases he may add his ten toes, and lump the rest. Simplicity, simplicity, simplicity! I say, let your affairs be as two or three, and not a hundred or a thousand; instead of a million count half a dozen, and keep your accounts on your thumb-nail."[5] His

---

[4]Christian Wiman, ed., *Joy: 100 Poems* (New Haven: Yale University Press, 2017), xii.
[5]Henry David Thoreau, *Walden and Other Writings*, ed. Brooks Atkinson (New York: Modern Library, 1992), 89.

formula—that the true cost of a thing is the amount of life it requires to be exchanged for it—is as pertinent now as ever.

There are many nonfiction items on this portion of my soul shelf that caught me by surprise. They help me to remember that a beautiful idea—in this case, the joy of simplicity—does not always have to be beautifully written to engage your mind and inspire you to change. But what all of these items have in common is that they touch that part of me that responds to God's original creative impulse to make order out of chaos. This goal is still aspirational for me, and for aspiration I need inspiration. I keep this quotation from William Morris on my door and firmly implanted in my mind when I declutter: "Have nothing in your houses that you do not know to be useful, or believe to be beautiful." To build the simplicity section of your shelf, start with the question, What helps me to recognize that it is possible to live in the present moment in peace and the fullness of joy?

Hanh, Thich Nhat, and H. H. the Dalai Lama. *Peace Is Every Step: The Path of Mindfulness in Everyday Life.* Edited by Arnold Kotler. New York: Bantam, 1992.

Hanh is a Zen monk with a lot of practice in the art of mindfulness. I have several of his books on my soul shelf. One need not be a Buddhist to see the value of practicing living in the present moment with simplicity and joy.

Kondo, Marie. *The Life-Changing Magic of Tidying Up: The Japanese Art of Decluttering and Organizing.* Berkeley: Ten Speed, 2014.

I'll admit that this austere book frightens me. Kondo is a minimalist if ever there was one, and she's got some crazy ideas here. Who doesn't keep their bottle of shampoo in the shower? But I have rarely read anything that inspires me to radically transform my living conditions, get out from under clutter, and breathe again as much as this book. And I've read a lot of books about clutter.

McRaven, William H. *Make Your Bed: Little Things That Can Change Your Life ... and Maybe the World.* New York: Grand Central, 2017.

Books about simplicity probably should be simple. This book is. It came out of a commencement address that Admiral McRaven gave at the University of Texas at Austin. He drew on his experience training as a Navy Seal to offer simple life lessons to the undergraduates. The first is to start your day with a task completed: make your bed. "Nothing can replace the strength and comfort of one's faith, but sometimes the simple act of making your bed can give you the lift you need to start your day and provide you the satisfaction to end it right."[6]

Norris, Kathleen. *The Quotidian Mysteries: Laundry, Liturgy and "Women's Work."* New York: Paulist Press, 1998.

This little gem was the originating text of my soul shelf. It is a perfect little readable book, full of poetic insight into why we cannot appreciate the quotidian and how to recover that appreciation.

Thoreau, Henry David. *Walden and Other Writings.* Edited by Brooks Atkinson. New York: Modern Library, 1992.

One of my favorite moments as a high school teacher came from teaching *Walden*. My sophomores hated this book that I cherish, and I was in despair. Since the school's property happened to include a nearby pond, I told the students to take nothing with them but paper and a pencil, and to spend the entire class period walking in silence around the pond. When we all gathered back in the classroom, one student said to me, "I don't think Thoreau is such a psycho anymore." I take my victories where I can. This was before smartphones, so one can only imagine how eye-opening such a silent walk would be today. Either way, I have always found the wisdom and beauty of *Walden* to be a balm to my soul.

Wiking, Meik. *The Little Book of Hygge: Danish Secrets to Happy Living.* New York: William Morrow, 2017.

See my February chapter for why this book is on my soul shelf. It doesn't take money or things to hygge your soul.

---

[6]William H. McRaven, *Make Your Bed: Little Things That Can Change Your Life ... and Maybe the World*, 2nd ed. (New York: Grand Central, 2017), 9.

LOVE

Of course, love is a huge concept, and the vagueness of the word in English offers no help. Here I'm hoping to encourage you to think about those things that stir you to love. Love is ecstatic: it moves us out of ourselves toward others. And since flourishing in our vocation requires a renewal of that love for students, this section is of paramount importance for all educators. It is not without good reason that one of the most famous teachers of all time, Socrates, conceived of teaching as an erotic invitation into a relationship with ideas and the holders of those ideas. This need not be a "don't stand so close to me" kind of sexual perversion. It is meant to help teachers to understand that students will and should be drawn to us if they sense that we have learned how to live the good life. As Parker Palmer reminds us, when we teach, we teach ourselves, whether we want to or not. It is possible to step into that passion without misleading them regarding the true object of their desire: God.

To build the love corner of your shelf, think about these questions: "What helps me to re-imagine other people, especially my students, as the reason why I am here?" and "What inspires me to come out of myself and cultivate a healthy love for others?"

Braveheart. Paramount Pictures.

My husband returns to this movie again and again for inspiration, and I know why he does. First of all, it helps us to recognize how much we take our freedom for granted. But it also inspires a deep dedication to a cause that will benefit others, which is what the teaching life is all about. These are the kinds of things that move us to action.

Dead Man Walking. PolyGram Filmed Entertainment.

Based on a true story of Sister Helen Prejean's work with an inmate on death row, this film is about the grit of love. Played by Susan Sarandon, Prejean says, "I want the last face you see in this world to be the face of

love, so you look at me when they do this thing. I'll be the face of love
for you." Wow. In truth, I have only seen this film twice because it is hard
to watch. But I wanted to put it on my list because it profoundly changed
my view of the death penalty. Love means remembering that it is his
kindness that leads us to repentance.

Leiva-Merikakis, Erasmo. *Fire of Mercy, Heart of the Word: Meditations on the Gospel According to Saint Matthew.* San Francisco: Ignatius, 1996.

If you want to remember why you love the Gospels of our Lord Jesus
Christ, you must read this book. Leiva-Merikakis's reading of Matthew is
creative without being unfaithful. It opened the book of Matthew to me,
and to greater love for Jesus and for others.

Lewis, C. S. *Till We Have Faces: A Myth Retold.* San Francisco: HarperOne, 2017.

Of course, there are several other books by Lewis that could be on this list
because he understood that the core battle of everyday was to get up and
turn your face toward God and see him as your heart's desire. This book
has a special place on my shelf because the protagonist, like me, had to
learn how misshapen her own desires had become.

The Lord of the Rings: Motion Picture Trilogy. New Line Cinema.

There have been half a dozen times that my husband and I have set aside
a whole day and evening to watch the extended versions of these three
films. This story reminds us that evil and destruction are easy, but love
requires courage, commitment, and long-suffering.

Mazzarella, Nicole. *This Heavy Silence: A Novel.* Brewster, MA: Paraclete, 2006.

This elegant and stirring novel was written by a friend I love deeply, so
of course it is on my soul shelf. The book you are holding in your hands
right now is in many ways a product of our friendship, but we are not
coauthors because I did not want to distract her from her own writing.
Just looking at this novel gives me joy because my friend is doing what
God created her to do. Her students are fortunate to have more of her
than they should, and this book reminds me that in many ways teaching

involves sacrificing one's passions in order to serve others. My father loved this novel so much that he keeps asking me when she is going to be finished with the next one. I can't wait, either.

The Mission: Original Soundtrack from the Motion Picture. Audio CD. Virgin Records, 1992.

This inspiring soundtrack, like the movie that it comes from, still opens my heart to want to serve others with more of myself.

Norris, Kathleen. The Cloister Walk. New York: Riverhead, 1997.

Although this book is not fundamentally about singleness, it gave me an irreplaceable gift at that difficult time of my life. Norris's keen observations about the Benedictine nuns and monks helped me to understand that the erotic energy of singleness is a gift that can be chastely given to others in a uniquely directed and focused love.

> As celibacy takes hold in a person, over the years, as monastic values supersede the values of the culture outside the monastery, celibates become people who can radically affect those of us out "in the world," if only because they've learned how to listen without possessiveness, without imposing themselves. With someone who is practicing celibacy well, we may sense that we're being listened to in a refreshingly deep way. And this is the purpose of celibacy, not to attain some impossibly cerebral goal mistakenly conceived as "holiness" but to make oneself available to others, body *and* soul.[7]

Amen.

Nouwen, Henri J. M. The Return of the Prodigal Son: A Story of Homecoming. New York: Image, 1994.

Nouwen struggled with the loneliness that comes from desiring too much from his relationships with others. If ever there was a person who learned how to retrain his desires toward their true object, it is Nouwen. Both this book and another favorite of mine, *The Inner Voice of Love,* are filled with wisdom that Nouwen gleaned from his personal and pastoral life. I have often taught and recommended this book to students.

---

[7]Kathleen Norris, *The Cloister Walk* (New York: Riverhead, 1997), 121.

I hope these selections from my shelf are an encouragement to you to build your own. I am also eager for my soul shelf to grow, so if you are inclined, please share your favorites with me. We have to survive the brutality of January and February no matter what, so we might as well do it with beauty, simplicity, and love.

February

Dealing with Deadwood Soul

I t is Monday, January 8, the first day of spring classes, and it is 4:00 p.m. I'm dead tired, but I'm writing this now because I want to remember how I felt. At various points throughout the day I had each one of the following thoughts and feelings, before and after I dragged myself through the usual first-day-of-class activities:

- Why am I doing this incredibly difficult job?
- I just want to go home and read in bed.
- Why do I live in the godforsaken, frozen state of Illinois?
- How can I be so tired on the first day of class?
- I'm becoming old and irrelevant.
- When is my next sabbatical?
- I don't care. About anything.
- I can't do this for another fifteen years.

I think that there is strength in knowing that thousands of other educators are hitting the same wall that you are, probably even at the exact moment you are reading this. In January and February, even more than in August, educators face significant motivational challenges. There is strength in remembering that it is, in fact, very difficult to get back into the groove of working at a breakneck pace when you just got a small taste of not doing it for a while. You should also rest assured that your fellow teachers (and your students) feel exactly the same way.

As I write these words, I am also about to face my fiftieth birthday. That's why I found myself thinking, for the first time that I can remember, that I can't do this job for another fifteen years. Even though I love my work most of the time, that thought still entered into my head, uninvited. Luckily it occurred to me that holding this inside was a very bad idea. So I texted it to my husband and friends. I texted BAJ, "I can't do anything. My motivational spring is broken." Saying it aloud was the best thing I could have done. It made me recognize that I will not always feel this way, and I just have to wait it out. It enabled the voice of wisdom and experience to speak back through me and say, "You don't have to get through the next fifteen years. You just have to get through today."

Call it what you will: your soul, spirit, psyche, or inner torque—whatever that thing is that makes you want to get up in the morning—sometimes that thing gets plum worn out. Sometimes it is the boredom of returning to the same mundane tasks. Sometimes it is that you had a very challenging holiday with family and did not have enough time to rest. Sometimes you are just not ready for classes. Sometimes you just don't want to have to get dressed and leave the house.

The bad news is that there is no ultimate answer to this. February is bleak. Spring break and the fourth quarter of the academic ball game seem distant. The amount of grading you have to do is increasing daily. You feel frustrated that you haven't had time to work on your own writing because you have been home caring for children with the flu. The students are tired also, which creates a downward spiral. They can't rely on you for your energy, and you cannot rely on them for theirs. Drudgery seems to be the order of the day.

The good news is that acknowledging that you feel this way can be very powerful. It is the first and most important step toward flourishing as a teacher. Out of the acknowledgment of this pattern and the conviction that I am not alone in my disdain for February, I have bits of seemingly contradictory advice for handling this month: survive it, hygge it, attack it.

Once again, the Christian calendar is there as both a challenge and a salve for our biggest needs and our perennial challenges. Although I admit that Lent is not my favorite season, it is also true that it can be a huge blessing for all three of these strategies.

SURVIVE FEBRUARY

Since I have been a Christian for more than forty years, I estimate that I've heard at least two thousand sermons in my lifetime. Of all of these, there is one that stands out for the force it has had in shaping my approach to my Christian life when it comes to handling this monstrosity we call February.

I need to give context. It was March 3, and I had finally made it to "spring" break. Anyone who lives in the upper Midwest knows that March—though we might see some warmer weather and the birds start coming back (hooray!)—is not spring. I've been known to shout to my nascent daffodils: "No! Go back! It's not safe here!" Since our spring break is so unspringlike, I made the decision several years ago that I would spend at least half of it in Los Angeles. But this particular spring break was different. My husband, who was in the process of being ordained as an Anglican priest, wanted to check out Nashotah House seminary. He asked me to accompany him. Nashotah House is a delightful, intentionally high-church Anglican seminary, complete with twice-daily, full-on services including Eucharist and prayers. There are loads of incense, vestments, rock-hard prayer benches, and *BCPs*, all designed to make any Anglo-Catholic drool.

But it's also located in Wisconsin. Needless to say, this was not my dream location for spring break after a long February. But I wanted to support my husband, and I did want to see the place myself, so there we were. That winter was a particularly cold and lengthy one in the upper Midwest, and so during the three days we visited the high temperature did not exceed fifteen degrees Fahrenheit. Friends, I admit that I grumbled. But it was sunny, and I was on break, so all was not lost. It was at one of the services that I heard the sermon. Actually, it was more like a very short homily. As a bit of a side note, I think that this ancient practice of delivering homilies would be a welcome alternative to the long and rambling American sermons I've heard over the years. Less really is more. Emily Dickinson kept the Sabbath at home because "God preaches, a noted Clergyman- / And the Sermon is never long." This particular Nashotah House homily was shorter than any I have ever heard. Of course I don't remember all of it, but the text was Matthew 24:13: "the one who endures to the end will be saved." The priest was an older man who had been teaching at Nashotah House for a very long time. He spoke about the harshness of this particular winter, the difficulties of the denials of Lent, and the bleakness that can sometimes enter the souls of even the most fervent among us. And he basically said that it is okay to *just endure it*. Are you experiencing a dark night of the soul right now? The one who endures to the end will be saved.

There was nothing sparkly or new or exciting about this homily. But it was exactly what I needed at that moment. The "long obedience in the same direction" that is the teaching life is often just this simple: it requires endurance. Grit. Long-suffering. Call it what you will, it means getting up in the morning when you'd rather stay in bed, putting on your clothes, and heading to the shop. I can't tell you how many times I've gotten up in February and said to myself, *Time to make the doughnuts.* The one who endures to the end will be saved.

At least half of the encouragement I got from that homily was from the honesty of the preacher. He was struggling with winter but was determined to be faithful to the promise of spring. Likewise we do well to remember that we are not alone in any of this. All educators everywhere are right there with you. This is why when I text BAJ that "my motivational spring is broken," she texts what she always does. This came on February fifteenth: "I am *so* there. I feel zapped of all ambition/motivation. Just want to watch movies. Seems a little early for this to hit. Shouldn't this be March?" For the record, she has never once texted me: "Oh wow, I'll pray for you!" as if she's having no problems making *her* doughnuts.

When it comes to hanging in there and enduring to the end, the Lenten season provides exactly this kind of group encouragement. Take some time every day to remember that we are a family. We are huddled together in a hard winter, sharing a time designed for us to remember the much more intense long-suffering of Jesus. For when we remember Jesus, we remember that there is an end to look forward to, and it is nearly here. Spring. Easter. The resurrection. They are coming.

HYGGE FEBRUARY

February should not be entirely about self-denial, as if there is some kind of virtue in complete abstention. To help me deal with the gloom of winter, I've had a lot of fun learning about and implementing the Danish practice of hygge. Pronounced *hoo-gah*, and adapted from a Norwegian word that means "well-being," it mostly means giving yourself a big, cozy hug by learning to enjoy the simple things about life during the dark winter months. If you find yourself feeling like you are in a dark corner right now and spring break seems distant, I encourage you to read some books or blogs on hygge and put some of the ideas into practice. It may seem silly to think that a cozy blanket and a roaring fire can help your mood, but that just might mean you are a cynical American workaholic. If you are willing to give it a try, here is my crash course on hygge.

My favorite treatment of what it means to live hygge is Meik Wiking's *The Little Book of Hygge*. The book is itself hygge: a small hardback of the perfect weight and size, with colorful pages that smell like books should smell. That's why it's on my soul shelf. Wiking has the world's best job: he's CEO of the Happiness Research Institute in Copenhagen. So take it from a Dane whose work it is to study happiness: intentionally creating your environment matters.

Hygge is about an atmosphere and an experience rather than things. It is about being with the people we love. A feeling of home. A feeling that we are safe, that we are shielded from the world and can allow ourselves to let our guard down. It might be having an endless conversation about the small or big things in life, enjoying the comfort of someone else's silent company, or simply enjoying a cup of tea by yourself.[1]

The key to hygge is that it cannot be purchased. Americans have a tendency to think that if we could just buy a list of items we read about in the magazine *Real Simple*, our lives would look and feel like that. But, according to Wiking, Danes are among the happiest people in the world because they do not try to find happiness in

---

[1]Meik Wiking, *The Little Book of Hygge: Danish Secrets to Happy Living* (New York: William Morrow, 2017), vi.

large-scale trips or expensive dinners on the town, nor do they try to buy hygge outside of a few small items like candles and tea. This is in part because they cannot afford it, as Denmark has one of the highest tax rates in the world. Apparently Danes take pride in being a country where the rich take responsibility for the well-being of the poor through the state. Imagine that.

It is also the case that most Danes do not become filthy rich because they would never dream of working at the pace that Americans have long accepted as normal and even required for success. When I read Arianna Huffington's book *Thrive*, I remember thinking about how it would never sell in Denmark. They just wouldn't understand it. It opens with Huffington explaining that her epiphany came when she was so tired from working all the time that she fell over and cracked her head on the coffee table. The fact that Huffington's book has sold millions of copies shows how Americans clearly idolize burning the candle at both ends and should be enough to make us want to move to Denmark. But Huffington did not invent the so-called third metric of success. She's just a high-powered executive who finally figured out that working nonstop is not commensurate with thriving. I'd rather take advice from the Danes, who seem to have never had this problem. It has never occurred to them to sacrifice everything to get to the top. Their workday is much shorter than ours, and vacations are longer and more, well, boring and unstructured. We have a lot to learn from this. The first key to hygge is letting go of thinking you've got to be working all the time. Do you have email on your phone? I'm talking to you, then. Delete that email app, pour yourself a mug of fragrant Earl Grey tea, and get your hygge on.

When Danes are asked what they associate with hygge, 85 percent of them will say candles. Candles are everywhere in Denmark, both at home and in the workplace—but they don't

burn them at both ends. Their prevalence led the American am-
bassador to note, "As an American, you think, *Fire hazard!* — how
can you possibly have an open flame in your classroom?"[2] I often
wish I could light candles in my office or my classroom, because
soft light is at the core of feeling hygge. Many of us work in anti-
septic offices and classrooms with fluorescent lights overhead. February is a good time to get hygge with your lighting. It is amazing
how much difference bringing your own lamps into the office can
make. I never turn on the overhead light in my office but rely
solely on my own lamps. That's hygge.

At home, of course, you can light as many candles as you want.
Just bear in mind that they do fill the air with more toxic particles
than smoking a cigarette does, so you'll want to air the room out
at some point. But I love to begin my short winter days by lighting
a candle in my study and end by lighting candles all over the
kitchen and family room. One of the things I insisted on when we
bought a new house here in Illinois was a real fireplace. It makes
a big difference about how I feel when the sun goes down in the
afternoon, the wind is howling, and it's so cold that the dog is
standing on two legs to do his business in the snow. My husband
and I agreed long ago that paying for firewood by the face cord
was a worthwhile winter expense. Find the things that help you
hygge, and invest in them with abandon.

The second major thing that Danes associate with hygge is hot
drinks. Mulled wine is of course the most hygge of all hot drinks,
but this won't do at work. I've already mentioned my coffee ritual,
but coffee is so important to hygge I want to dwell on the topic a bit
more. When my husband was underemployed and working at Starbucks to have something to do, he learned a lot about coffee — and

---

[2]Wiking, *Little Book of Hygge*, 2.

human nature. Regular customers were usually great, but occasionally you have regulars who just expect you to know them. One such guy was known as "the perfect cup of coffee guy." He'd pull up to the drive-through and say, "I'd like the perfect cup of coffee." It was annoying enough to expect all the baristas to remember his order, but readers, what he wanted was not really coffee. First, it was decaf. What's the point? Then he wanted two packets of Splenda, cinnamon dolce powder, and steamed soymilk. Definitely not my perfect cuppa. But hygge is finding your perfect cup and treating yourself to it. Coffee is the evangelical drug, the Dutch gasoline that has fueled generations of hard workers. My husband knows a priest whose congregation borrows their building from a Seventh-Day Ad-

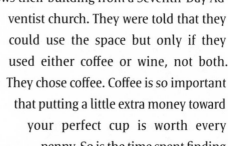

ventist church. They were told that they could use the space but only if they used either coffee or wine, not both. They chose coffee. Coffee is so important that putting a little extra money toward your perfect cup is worth every penny. So is the time spent finding the best way to prepare it and the blend you favor. Since I love my coffee smooth, creamy, and not

Figure 7.1. Chemex

bitter, my two favorite ways to prepare are cold brew and Chemex.

At Starbucks it's always a grande flat white with four shots. But I'll drink it any way, especially with a friend. Often BAJ will brew a French press pot of our favorite coffee—Peet's Major Dickason's blend—and do our secret knock on my door. That's hygge, and it helps in February.

My afternoon tea is almost as important to me as my morning coffee. As C. S. Lewis famously wrote, "You can never get a cup of

tea large enough or a book long enough to suit me."[3] Since I
drink a hot mug of tea every afternoon, usually between 2:00
and 3:00 p.m., I want to get the best loose-leaf tea I can to increase my enjoyment of it. Because I drink my tea with cream, I
like it black and strong. My current favorite is Paris Breakfast by
Mariage Frères. Incidentally, if you are still using those paltry
American tea bags, you have not really had tea. Buy high-quality
loose-leaf, and brew it in a device, like Adagio Tea's ingenuiTEA,
that allows the leaves to expand properly and the tea to drain
out of the bottom. And don't forget mindfulness. We can either
drink tea like a worker craving caffeine or drink it like it is the
special treat that it is. I love this quotation about concentration
from Thich Nhat Hanh:

> Suppose you are offered a cup of tea, very fragrant, very good
> tea. If your mind is distracted, you cannot really enjoy the tea.
> You have to be mindful of the tea, you have to be concentrated
> on it, so the tea can reveal its fragrance and wonder to you. That
> is why mindfulness and concentration are such sources of hap-
> piness. That's why a good practitioner knows how to create a
> moment of joy, a feeling of happiness, at any time of the day.[4]

We can also do things to make our classes more hygge. If you
are thinking about having students to your home for dinner, now
is the time to do it. They can't have candles, a fireplace, or pets in
the dorms, and these things help them too. Students also appreciate even small gestures of hospitality like bringing in coffee on
a blustery February day, or preparing some homemade treats. I'm
not good at this, but I am trying to improve.

---

[3] C. S. Lewis, *On Stories: And Other Essays on Literature* (New York: HarperOne, 2017), ix.
[4] Thich Nhat Hanh, *Your True Home: The Everyday Wisdom of Thich Nhat Hanh: 365 Days of Practical, Powerful Teachings from the Beloved Zen Teacher*, ed. Melvin McLeod (Boston: Shambhala, 2011), 6.

Can you move your class to a different location? One sunny February I held class in the biology department's greenhouse, and we were all joyfully stripping off our sweaters and socks by the end of it. We can also experiment with lighting and other technology in our classrooms. When I was walking down the hall during exam period one winter, I saw that the professor had put up a video of a crackling fireplace on the large screen at the front of the class. Amazon video has other high-definition video streams, including mesmerizing clips of the northern lights. Putting up something like this during an exam is a small gesture, but it is still hygge. Anything that you can do to help students to feel safe and at home in your classroom will be energy well spent. Thing 10: Classroom creativity pays off in energy what it costs in content.

NINJA FEBRUARY

While Advent is a season of waiting, Lent is a season of repentance. And repentance is decidedly not hygge. It cannot be passive or cozy. It involves turning away from bad practices and embracing healthy ones. The reason we often give up things—chocolate, alcohol, meals, social media—is to acknowledge that we have gotten far too accustomed to satiating our every desire. The satiation has made us comfortable and lazy. So while intentionally going hygge has a time and place in February and March, so does intentionally going ninja. Spiritual ninja, that is.

If you have ever seen the television series *American Ninja Warrior*, you will know what I mean. Hundreds of men and women train for months to compete in a single event that comes down to less than five minutes per contestant. They have to complete an obstacle course that involves tremendous upper body strength, dexterity, and mental tenacity. The ninjas give themselves funny names—there is even a lay Catholic who calls himself the "Papal

Ninja" — and they bring their fans with their matching T-shirts. It is surprisingly inspiring to watch.

No one would ever go to that competition without disciplined training for it. This training is lengthy, regular, arduous, and un-rewarded at the time of its occurrence. So I now think about Lent as training to be a spiritual ninja. It seems silly, but by giving themselves warrior names, the ninjas get even more focused. They have to live up to being the "Princess Warrior Ninja" or the "Phoenix Ninja." Thinking of myself as a spiritual ninja works es-pecially well for me because often what I need most in my spiritual life is some kind of physical discipline. Having become soft and lazy during the holidays, I usually need to increase the amount of exercise I get or to double down on healthy eating. So I often attack February by adding a new exercise routine, one that I haven't tried before or haven't done in a long time. If you have ever contemplated joining a planned routine like Orangetheory, CrossFit, or the Dailey Method, now would be a great time. The change in routine yields as big a boost of energy as the routine itself does. Thing 11: Exercise always helps. Even a tiny bit of ex-ercise. If you don't believe me, just try it. Go to your gym's inside track right now and do sprints. This doesn't need to take more than twelve minutes. When your blood pumps oxygen to your brain, it changes everything. Similarly, if you've thought of trying Whole30, or just eliminating sugar or carbs, Lent is for you. You can even match it with the Lenten season and make it Whole40. At the very least, the discipline will make you feel better, give you more energy, and help February to be less bleak.

Ultimately, the reason for Lenten physical disciplines is not to compete in some contest, but to create space for spiritual growth and renewal. We have all experienced how a small physical change can produce energy for other, more important changes.

To me, that's the purpose of Lent and its focus on self-examination. Is there a better season in our lives to deliberately increase prayer time, to slow down long enough to listen to God, especially as he might be speaking through others? I have found that choosing a different text to pray with and journal about for each Lenten season can help me to be more open to what God is trying to show me. One year, I discovered a particularly poignant combination of texts to pray through and chew on. I made a point of asking God to teach me how to abide in Christ, according to his words from John 15:

> I am the true vine, and my Father is the vinegrower. He removes every branch in me that bears no fruit. Every branch that bears fruit he prunes to make it bear more fruit. You have already been cleansed by the word that I have spoken to you. Abide in me as I abide in you. Just as the branch cannot bear fruit by itself unless it abides in the vine, neither can you unless you abide in me. I am the vine, you are the branches. Those who abide in me and I in them bear much fruit, because apart from me you can do nothing. Whoever does not abide in me is thrown away like a branch and withers; such branches are gathered, thrown into the fire, and burned. If you abide in me, and my words abide in you, ask for whatever you wish, and it will be done for you. My Father is glorified by this, that you bear much fruit and become my disciples. As the Father has loved me, so I have loved you; abide in my love. If you keep my commandments, you will abide in my love, just as I have kept my Father's commandments and abide in his love. I have said these things to you so that my joy may be in you, and that your joy may be complete. (Jn 15:1-11)

I especially tried to create silence around these words so that I could listen to God remind me that he loves me and that his joy can be mine. While I was working through this passage, I also happened upon a book that changed my thinking about how to abide in Christ — even though Christ is not specifically named in it. It is called *Slowing Down to the Speed of Life*, and it powerfully and simply reminded me that it is not our circumstances, but rather our thoughts about those circumstances, that create our reality. If I'm in a long line in a grocery store, I have a choice either to be agitated and annoyed, or to be patient and loving toward others. Because of the perspective I have that comes from Christ in me — the hope of glory — I *always* have the choice to respond rather than to react. It is very simple. The first step is to notice what I am thinking. The next is to notice that I can change that thought. This must be part of what St. Paul had in mind when he wrote that "we take every thought captive to obey Christ" (2 Cor 10:5). It's a discipline and a practice, and it requires slowing down long enough to dispassionately examine the thoughts I'm actually having in any situation. For example, when I go to the gym do I think: "Ugh. Time to go exercise," or do I think "Thank God I have the ability and opportunity to exercise"? The truth is that our thoughts are every bit as habitual as brushing our teeth or fixing a cup of coffee in the morning. When I wait long enough it becomes completely clear that the choice of what to think and how to respond in every situation in life is mine and mine alone. Thanks be to God.

Finally, if you are spiritually fatigued this February, try mixing up your training regime a little bit. Listen to an inspiring podcast, especially while exercising, or join that small group you've been thinking about joining. Are there some books that you've been wanting to read? Set up a consistent plan to give yourself time to read them — maybe during the time you would have watched television. There are all kinds of wonderful books out there on how to encounter the deep spiritual challenges of the season. I've recommended some below. If your college has a faculty development day in February like we do, try going with gusto this year, intent on encouraging others who may be struggling. Or if you always dutifully go, slouching toward what you suspect won't help much, skip it this year and spend the time taking a long and invigorating prayer walk. Mix it up. The point is that sometimes doing old-hat things even a tiny bit differently can create an unexpected avalanche of new energy and joy.

I cannot tell a lie. When I think of February, I'm mostly grateful that it is a short month. It is cold, dark, snowy, and has the crappy pseudo-holidays of President's Day and Valentine's Day. But I have also learned to be grateful for Lent, which contains the promise of the resurrection. Lent and winter are hard, but sometimes that is what we really need. This is why I have trained myself to think of Lent as the spiritual equivalent of opening the windows when it is very cold outside. If you have never opened your windows on a winter day, you should do it. Not only is it important to air the house out regularly (especially if you've overdone the hygge candles), but the fresh air blows in through the curtains and fills your lungs with deliciousness. I often feel like I can see the stale molecules in the air being replaced by fresh ones. Lent is like that. Old habits can be seen for the stale sustenance that they are, and the new ones are an invitation to the Holy Spirit to clean us out.

FOR ADDITIONAL ENCOURAGEMENT

Carlson, Richard, and Joseph Bailey. *Slowing Down to the Speed of Life: How to Create a More Peaceful, Simpler Life from the Inside Out.* HarperOne, 2009.

As I mentioned above, this simple book continues to be a game changer for me. Although it is not written from an explicitly Christian perspective, it is consonant in every way with learning how to abide moment by moment in the love and joy of Christ Jesus.

Crosby, Cindy. *Waiting for Morning: Hearing God's Voice in the Darkness.* Grand Rapids: Baker, 2001.

Written by a fellow Illinois winter survivor, this delightful little book will give you the feeling of being outdoors when the weather makes that impossible. Since it owes a lot to Thoreau and Dillard — and since I know Cindy to be a gentle and wise woman — I can't help but love it.

Foster, Richard J. *Celebration of Discipline: The Path to Spiritual Growth.* Special Anniversary Edition. San Francisco: HarperOne, 2018.

A classic for more than forty years for good reason. Foster helps us to enter a number of different ancient spiritual disciplines, including fasting, prayer, and service, and explains why they are so important and transformative.

Hanh, Thich Nhat. *Your True Home: The Everyday Wisdom of Thich Nhat Hanh: 365 Days of Practical, Powerful Teachings from the Beloved Zen Teacher.* Edited by Melvin McLeod. Boston: Shambhala, 2011.

At this time of year, I find small, daily readings to be particularly useful. This one helps me to stay in the present moment, even when I'm cold and tired.

Neuhaus, Richard John. *Death on a Friday Afternoon: Meditations on the Last Words of Jesus from the Cross.* New York: Basic Books, 2001.

Written by the former editor of *First Things*, I've returned to this book during many a Lenten season. "If what Christians say about Good Friday is true, then it is, quite simply, the truth about everything," Neuhaus writes. A very wise book to read and reread. I can't help thinking that Fr. Neuhaus would have enjoyed watching the Papal Ninja.

Russell, Helen. *The Year of Living Danishly: Uncovering the Secrets of the World's Happiest Country.* London: Icon, 2016.

This little book will keep you laughing as it follows Russell's efforts to adapt to Danish culture.

8

March

Dr. Jekyll and Mrs. Hyde

This is the chapter that nearly wasn't.

It was nearing the end of March, so naturally I said to myself, *This would be a good time to write my March chapter.* The problem was that I had nothing. No motivation to do anything—at all. I didn't want to teach my classes, go to committee meetings, answer email, or write. It was all I could do to just get out of bed in the morning with a smirky substitute for a smile on my face. So, when I felt like I should be able to write this chapter (which I had been saving, like a child saves broccoli, for last), I sent a text to my writing group. "I need to write one more chapter to get a complete draft. March. But I can't get myself to do anything."

Encouragement and understanding flowed from my friends as usual. They were all in the exact same place. The best reply I got was from BAJ: "Title the chapter 'March,' and leave it blank. Everyone will understand." I almost did it.

I do feel like a big, exhausted blank most of every March, even after spring break. But I couldn't just write about that, either, because that's the subject of my February and April chapters—and pretty soon my readers will think that my motivational spring breaks every spring semester, all semester long. But if I'm being honest, that is true more often than not. When it's mid-summer and I think back on February, March, and April, I think, *What a slog*. I am amazed what the lack of sun does to me and how much the pace I must keep grinds me down. So if you are reading this in March, the main thing I want to say to you is, "Hang in there." This, too, shall pass. Reread the February chapter for ideas on how to handle this, or skip ahead to April to remind yourself that Easter will get here eventually.

What I am going to do in this chapter is confess my failures. I want to keep it real. The fact is, even success doesn't always feel or look like success, especially from the inside. Sometimes it is only my good habits that keep me going — and by "going," I mean getting out of bed and doing my job at a bare minimum. But as everyone knows, there are bad habits crouching and waiting to devour all the good ones. I've been there too. You've met Dr. Jekyll. In this chapter, you will meet Mrs. Hyde.

The famous story of Dr. Jekyll and Mr. Hyde is familiar to everyone and read by very few. Dr. Jekyll basically offloads his bad self by way of a potion, creating Mr. Hyde. He lives a double existence, disciplined by day and profligate by night. The problem is that Mr. Hyde's personality eventually takes over the show, and Dr. Jekyll dies by way of a suicidal Mr. Hyde. It's a sad story, but for the perceptive reader, the sadness is revealed early on. Dr. Jekyll's doom is sure when he proclaims to Utterson that "the moment I choose, I can be rid of Mr. Hyde." Nope. The fact is, we don't get to choose to stop any bad behavior once and for all. Here's why.

BE WILLPOWER WISE

There has been a lot of recent research into the idea of willpower, and the findings have been consistent. Willpower exists in a way closer to the Victorians' understanding of it as a virtue rather than

Freud's understanding of it as an illusion. That's the good news. The bad news is that every one of us has a limited supply of it. Willpower is kind of like a single muscle we use over and over, and we live in a world that constantly requires us to exercise it. As Baumeister and Tierney explain, thousands of test subjects in and out of the laboratory have proven that you have a finite amount of willpower that becomes depleted as you use it, and you use the same stock of willpower for all manner of tasks.[1]

The primary reason for willpower depletion, especially for those of us in any kind of judgment-making professions like law, management, or education, is something called decision fatigue. The more decisions you have to make throughout the day, even simple ones, the less willpower you have to resist that glass of wine or pint of ice cream in the evening. In other words, being an effective Dr. Jekyll by day is actually what empowers your insidious Mr. Hyde by night.

To explain how powerfully depleting decision fatigue is, Baumeister and Tierney report on some pretty scary research involving judges making decisions about parole for prisoners. A team of psychologists studied more than one thousand decisions made by an Israeli parole board over the course of ten months. Granting parole is both a very serious and a seriously subjective decision. If you grant parole, you give the prisoners their freedom and save the taxpayers' money. You also risk recidivism by the prisoner. If you deny parole, you cost the system money and consign the prisoner to serve more time. Needless to say, this is a burden. On average, the judges granted parole to about one-third of the prisoners overall. But here's what else the psychologists discovered. The prisoners who appeared early in the morning received parole 70

---

[1] Roy F. Baumeister and John Tierney, *Willpower: Rediscovering the Greatest Human Strength* (New York: Penguin, 2012), 35.

percent of the time, while the ones who appeared at the end of the day received it less than 10 percent of the time. The researchers also found that there was an increase in parole granting after the judges took a break or ate lunch to replenish their glucose stores by eating. Here's how Baumeister and Tierney explain these findings:

> Judging is hard mental work. As the judges made one decision after another, their brains and bodies used up glucose, that crucial component of willpower that we discussed earlier. Whatever their personal philosophy—whether they were known for being tough on crime or sympathetic to the potential for rehabilitation—they had fewer available mental resources to make further decisions. And so, apparently, they tended to go for the less risky choice (for themselves, anyway).[2]

There might be other psychological factors at play here. Maybe the judges had an unconscious inner limit on how many paroles they would grant. But the fact is that this is not an isolated discovery. Experiments repeatedly reveal the results of decision fatigue. They also clearly indicate that the more of these kinds of decisions you make during the day, the less likely you are able to make hard choices during the evening, like not drinking that glass of wine or eating that bag of potato chips.

It would be interesting to run this kind of experiment on teachers who grade papers. Assessment involves making countless truly subjective decisions—and usually completely independently. It is exhausting, and we need to remember that. I've worked diligently at trying to reduce the stress of grading papers and move the whole operation from a lose-lose one to a win-win one. I still have a long way to go. As I mentioned in chapter one, I've stopped assigning research essays that come due at the end of the semester

---

[2]Baumeister and Tierney, *Willpower*, 98.

for many of my classes. I get mean when I grade a stack of papers. I've streamlined my grading process as much as I can by having students submit electronic copies of their papers in PDF. I store them in a note-taking application called Notability until I am ready to assess them, usually early Monday, Wednesday, or Friday morning. When it comes time, I use my Apple pencil to mark directly on the document, and then I use the recording feature to attach a verbal message for each student. This helps me to be much more nuanced in my comments, and it prevents them from overlooking the good things I have to say and focusing only on the areas for improvement. I used to not give grades on papers at all because students saw the grade and ignored the comments. With this recording system, I can tell them their grade at the end of my little voicemail, and I can say it sweetly with all kinds of qualifications. One day I may return to not giving grades at all; I'm still experimenting. But since research indicates that some students are motivated by low grades to do well and some are motivated by high grades, just giving a grade and a few handwritten comments that justify it is the worst possible strategy for everyone involved. Whatever strategy you choose, take some time to explain it to the students. Intentionality is always key.

But of course, grading isn't the only decision-heavy work that educators do, especially humanities professors. We write, and hopefully we write a lot. After reading *Willpower* it became clear to me why writers struggle with alcohol so much. Having a drinking problem is practically a rite of passage for literary artists. Raymond Carver, Andre Dubus, Mary Karr, Denis Johnson, Elizabeth Bishop — the list goes on and on. Is there any profession that consistently demands thousands of decisions per hour as writing does? Part of the reason writing is so difficult is because you have to *decide*, a word that, like *homicide*, has "killing" at its root. When you choose a topic, you kill off all other topics. When you choose a thesis, you kill off all other theses. This is the same with paragraphs, sentences, and words. It's a kind of exhaustion by decision.

So where does that leave us at the literal end of the day? For most of the work that educators do, the shot of bourbon not only feels like the perfect reward for a tough day, but it also helps us to let go of everything that made it tough in the first place. Alcohol relaxes the fatigued willpower muscle almost immediately. Mr. Hyde gets in your bloodstream, kills some brain cells, lessens your inhibitions — and pours you another drink. The appeal is precisely in the letting go. "Contrary to popular stereotype, alcohol doesn't increase your impulse to do stupid or destructive things; instead, it simply removes restraints," explain Baumeister and Tierney. "It lessens self-control in two ways: by lowering blood glucose and by reducing self-awareness. Therefore, it mainly affects behaviors marked by inner conflict, as when part of you wants to do something and part of you does not, like having sex with the wrong person, spending too much money, getting into a fight — or ordering another drink, and then another."[3]

What I am beginning to learn from all of this is that what my personal Mrs. Hyde wants from the glass of wine is the permission to stop making hard decisions. If I drink in the evening, I do it because I unconsciously know that it will reduce my inhibitions and "allow" me to eat Tostitos with that lethal queso dip. Since Dr. Jekyll has decided not to eat Tostitos, I simply invite Mrs. Hyde to get rid of her. Needless to say, this is a bad habit. I told you I would be honest with you here.

Who will save us from this body of death? Praise be to the Lord Jesus Christ (Rom 7:24-25) — and the power of good habits. I don't

---

[3]Baumeister and Tierney, *Willpower*, 169.

mean to be flippant here: it is essential to call out to the Lord for help, and there is no substitute for surrendering to God. But it is also useful, as I mentioned in chapter two, to investigate all of your habits from the inside. The only way to get rid of bad habits is to identify their cue and reward system, and then to find a Christ-centered, life-giving replacement for them. This is, of course, hard to figure out and much harder to implement. When it comes to things like alcohol, Baumeister and Tierney recommend finding where you need to place your "bright line" and then sticking to it. A bright line is a decision you make ahead of time about something you will or will not do. If you know that drinking one glass of wine will tempt you to drink another so that you can hear the call of the Tostito, your bright line is either to stop drinking altogether or to make a firm commitment to having no alcohol during the week. This is the bright line I have drawn in this area of my life. But I have also learned why it is so hard to stick to, and what causes me to fail. Knowledge of this kind is real power.

DECREASE DECISION FATIGUE

Since we cannot change the decision-heavy nature of the work that we do, it is important to build systems that demand fewer decisions in areas where we don't need to make them. I think this is particularly important when it comes to the amount of start-up energy that decision-heavy tasks require. If you have to trust yourself to decide to sit down to write whenever you get a chunk of time, you will never get that chunk of time. Something else will always be more urgent, appealing, or easier to do. But if you make a decision ahead of time to write every Tuesday between 6:00 a.m. and 1:00 p.m., and you protect that time, you will get a lot done. The prolific Victorian novelist Anthony Trollope apparently worked exactly in this fashion (although, having a wife and a cook, it was easier to set aside time every day). I think the same is true for grading, as I have already indicated. You have to find what works best for you, and stick to it until it becomes like brushing your teeth.

There are other areas where pre-deciding can be a huge benefit in reducing decision fatigue in an educator's life. For example, for the last three years I have been wearing a work uniform. I have never been interested in fashion, and when I recognized that I was wasting my precious willpower muscle trying to decide what to wear every day, I went minimal. I would love to be able to wear my regalia with shorts and a tank top under it, but alas, that's not done here. So instead I have a few very simple pieces and accessories that I mix and match and wear to class. It's boring, but I love it. If I could stop gaining weight (a story for another day), I would have the smallest closet-space need of any woman in the country. I've even started to mention my work uniform to my students so that I know they know I'm not playing the fashion game and am just here to teach. I know that this approach is not for everyone. If you get pleasure out of choosing your look for the day, then by all means, go for it.

Another thing that I have done to reduce decision-making fatigue is to plan things I have not been in the habit of planning. I'm not a great planner, but it is amazing how much easier life is when I do. For example, consider meals. We spend so much of our precious willpower making decisions about what and how to feed ourselves and our families. If you are responsible for the cooking in your house, it pays off to sit down once a week and work out your grocery list and recipes in advance. Even if you cannot afford to hire Trollope's cook, you can outsource this work in a variety of ways. For example, I love SavingDinner.com. Leanne Ely has created a business out of providing meal plans for every type of diet, and the times when I've subscribed to her plans have been a joy. I stopped only because my husband and son would eat tacos every day of the week and didn't care about the variety as much as I did, so it wasn't worth the work. I've never tried a home meal–component delivery service such as HelloFresh, Blue Apron, or Purple Carrot, but I've heard good things about them. If you can afford this, it would be a substantial reduction in time spent shopping and in decision fatigue. That's a win-win.

All kinds of situations benefit from advance planning. And one of the most important things to plan for is real rest.

ENJOY SPRING BREAK

For most of us, March does at least contain the shiny promised land known as spring break. As we all know, this time away from class is essential for the mental and physical health of students and educators alike. The only problem is that we usually don't take a break. Compounding the problem is the fact that for college professors, our break often does not line up with that of our children. When my husband was working as a philosophy professor at Trinity Christian College, his break was on the second week in March; mine was on the first week; and our son's was on the third. This left us scrambling for childcare, which compounded the exhaustion factor. As I watched my faculty friends, I noticed that we all tended to approach the break in the same counterproductive way. Since we can't go anywhere, we usually use the extra time to pretend to work, and then we feel guilty about our lack of productivity. There are a number of reasons for this, but the primary one is the momentum myth I will discuss in chapter ten. We always think we will have more energy (and time) than we will actually have, and the mismatch is what makes us miserable. Thing 4: Don't try to work when you are exhausted.

After a few years of teaching, I finally recognized that I was returning from my supposed break even more exhausted then I was when I crawled into it. So I decided to approach it differently. I started planning to take a real break instead pushing myself to be productive. As I mentioned earlier, I don't give traditional midterm exams or papers. I also make a point of not assigning extra work to the students. Then I milk this fact for all it's worth: "Have a great break. If you have time, you might want to read the longer novel that we will be reading later, but you don't have to. When I was a sophomore I was assigned both *David Copperfield* and *Don Quixote* to read over my spring break, so enjoy knowing you don't have to do that!" (By the way, that story is true. I sat in the hammock at my aunt and uncle's house in Washington, DC, and read all week. I loved it, but I was also destined to become a college professor. Most of our students are not headed for that, and we need to allow them to rest.)

Trust me: if you are in this work for the long haul, you need to rest too. Why do we tend to forget that during the days of his public ministry—and in the prime of his life—Jesus dismissed the crowds and went by himself to a quiet place to get some rest? (Mt 14:13). The best decision I made with regard to spring break was when I decided that I would go to Los Angeles every year for a long weekend, usually the first weekend of the break. By "long weekend," I mean *long*: I leave Friday after my last class and stay until Wednesday. My closest friend from college lives in L.A., and staying with her is a treat to my soul. The sunshine saves me from the despair that sets in when Illinois cruelly withholds spring from us, as it always does, year after year. I know that such an escape is a luxury that many faculty members with young children cannot enjoy, but if it is at all possible for you to plan something like this, I encourage you to do so. It is worth every penny to me to sit in the sun and restore my soul. I return invigorated. I can usually plan one or two solid writing days and tackle the inevitable mound of catch-up work for the end of the week.

Usually, but not always. What happens if you are not energized and inspired to teach even after you take a real break? I've been there too. If you cannot get as much done as you wanted to, and your Mrs. Hyde is nagging at you with Tostitos and wine, remember to give yourself some grace. In the immortal words of Kenny Rogers, "You gotta know when to fold 'em."

After all, I didn't write this chapter in March. I wrote it in June.

FOR ADDITIONAL ENCOURAGEMENT

Baumeister, Roy F., and John Tierney. *Willpower: Rediscovering the Greatest Human Strength.* New York: Penguin, 2012.

Filled with a lot of great, eye-opening research.

McGonigal, Kelly. *The Willpower Instinct: How Self-Control Works, Why It Matters, and What You Can Do to Get More of It.* New York: Avery, 2013.

This is probably my favorite of all the willpower books I've read because it is based on a popular class that McGonigal teaches. It is filled with the nitty-gritty, down-to-earth advice we all need to change those deep-seated habits.

Smith, James K. A. *You Are What You Love: The Spiritual Power of Habit.* Grand Rapids: Brazos, 2016.

There's nothing new here, but if you have not taken the time to consider the fact that what you expose yourself to on a regular basis is shaping you spiritually, then you need to read this book. Jamie is a brilliant philosopher who knows how to bring the best of the big ideas down to the rest of us.

Warren, Tish Harrison. *Liturgy of the Ordinary: Sacred Practices in Everyday Life.* Downers Grove, IL: InterVarsity Press, 2016.

Another excellent book about the power of everyday decisions and observances. Tish, an Anglican priest, follows a typical day from sunup to sundown. She is not afraid to admit to her inner Mrs. Hyde.

April

The Cruelest Month:
Live for Easter

pril is the cruellest month, breeding
Lilacs out of the dead land, mixing
Memory and desire, stirring
Dull roots with spring rain.

In 1922 T. S. Eliot opened his poem "The Waste Land" with these despairing and ironic words. It would be five years before his conversion to the Church of England, and in these years he could see with clarity the condition of the modern person in a world that had declared the death of God—isolated, trapped by unsatisfied desires, and without hope for redemption. Eliot knew that April meant Easter in the Christian tradition, but in 1922 he could see the life-giving rain only as cruel. It stirs with an empty promise of renewal that he had worked so hard to numb. "Don't stir me up with false hopes," these lines seem to say. "The renewal of spring never sticks. Growth is just a cruel hoax."

Eliot would come later to accept and celebrate a central paradox of life in Christ: growth hurts, but in that pain is our redemption. Our hope is real.

I find it cause for both celebration and chagrin that March and April are the hardest months in the lives of educators. We are

usually overworked, overcommitted, and overtired. The school calendar is packed full of wonderful lectures by visiting scholars, but
we have no time or energy to attend them. We often feel stuck,
wondering what happened to the writing we had hoped to do. We
can glimpse the proverbial light at the end of the tunnel, but it
still feels so far away.

Furthermore, we are broken human beings, just like our students. It is likely that in our personal lives, Lent has been a season
of repentance. It has been like pre-spring or "just spring" in that
as the light of Christ and the rain of his word stirred our dull roots,
we began to see what needs to change. Maybe there was a rock in
the way. We asked God for the strength and courage to move it. We
said to him that we needed his light—he gave it, and we are
groping now with those first tiny tendrils that reach up out of the
dirt toward the source of life. We are tender, tentative. We are
finding out what a character in Toni Morrison's *Beloved* discovered,
that "anything dead coming back to life hurts."[1]

In these pre-spring days, which can seem so long and so difficult, I find great comfort in the fact that the church calendar
teaches us exactly what to do. We must fix our eyes on the end:
the resurrection of Christ. Easter is the reward. No matter how
meaningless and redundant our lives have grown to feel, Easter
represents the very real hope of new life that is ours in Christ
Jesus. It is our reward for trusting that God will bring to life what
we would have left for dead. Let's encourage each other with the
words of Scripture, "Listen, I will tell you a mystery! We will not
all die, but we will all be changed, in a moment, in the twinkling
of an eye, at the last trumpet. For the trumpet will sound, and the
dead will be raised imperishable, and we will be changed. For this

---

[1] Toni Morrison, *Beloved* (New York: Vintage, 2004), 42.

perishable body must put on imperishability, and this mortal body must put on immortality" (1 Cor 15:51-53). In short, during the monotony of February, March, and April, we must find a way to live in the hope of Easter. The snow that has been on the ground since January will melt. The flowers will bloom again. We will get the alleluia back, and it will be glorious. But yes, we need to get there first, and there is pain along the way.

As I mentioned in chapter six, Kathleen Norris's *Quotidian Mysteries* is on my soul shelf. Norris has tremendous insight into the true nature of acedia, a sin that has been misnamed "sloth."[2] Most Americans know only that is one of the seven deadly sins and assume that it means being lazy. But that is not what acedia is. Acedia is a feeling of lethargy that comes over you, depriving you of the desire to do even simple things like washing your hair. I have always loved the term *listless* because it captures acedia well. *List* is a Middle English word for desire or appetite. When you are without list, you aren't moved by anything. Your *eros*, your passion, has dissolved. The nautical term *list* refers to leaning to one side, usually from imbalanced cargo. I like to think of it this way: whether you are a big ship or a tiny pirogue, if you are listless, you are not leaning into anything. You are adrift, and your engines are dead in the water.

Paradoxically, acedia doesn't come from being lazy. It usually comes from having worked too hard, having revved one's engines to burnout. Those of us with a perfectionist streak, who are trying to live out the "Be All That You Can Be" US Army commercials I remember from years ago, suffer from acedia the most. We have lost perspective on what really matters. Norris explains that "workaholism is the opposite of humility, and to an unhumble literary

---

[2] She has also written another book on acedia called *Acedia and Me*.

workaholic such as myself, morning devotions can feel useless, not nearly as important as getting about my business early in the day." The kind of pride that makes us think we are better than the quotidian is the core of the problem. "I know from bitter experience that when I allow busy little doings to fill that precious time of early morning, when contemplation might flourish, I open the doors to the demon of acedia."[3] Acedia is the demon our workaholic pride deserves, for when it sets in, it kills off the desire to do anything. "Who's the big wig now?" it asks as it laughs. So when April's early spring rain begins to stir our dulled roots, it feels like fire. "Just let us stay asleep," we beg. Just let us go through the motions, drag to the finish.

My favorite part of Norris's reflection on acedia is her description of what happens to her when winter finally breaks its hold in South Dakota. I didn't think anyone else could possibly struggle with this kind of acedia:

> Spring can seem to me like "a blind green wall," an implacable force stirring things into life that has grown comfortably dormant. It is one of the perversities of my interior makeup that I so often become depressed just as winter makes its turn into spring, and the longed-for moment arrives; the weather turns pleasant, and one can walk out of doors without bundling up. But unbundling means exposure, a kind of vulnerability, and I seldom feel ready for it when that first balmy day arrives. Instead, I resist the good news of spring, lurking inside my house as if it is still winter. My spirit suffers, my garden languishes, and my perennial flowers and herbs must struggle on their own with the encroaching weeds.[4]

---

[3] Kathleen Norris, *The Quotidian Mysteries: Laundry, Liturgy and "Women's Work"* (New York: Paulist Press, 1998), 25.
[4] Norris, *Quotidian Mysteries*, 36.

I have felt exactly the same way. The listlessness that sets into one's soul during the winter weeks is hard to overcome. So what is to be done? I think the first thing to do is to recognize that for most of us, acedia is the result of prolonged fatigue and stress. Take Norris's advice, and don't jump right into the work of the day as if the world would shut down without you. Furthermore, if you have a regular pattern of burnout in March or April, then you would do well to plan for it. Remembering that acedia is not laziness, we all need to relearn how to play hooky. Build TBA days into your syllabus and use them, judiciously, to cancel class on occasion. Administrators may not like to hear this, but faculty members really do need one or two mental health days per semester. We get stuck in grueling ruts because we are doing the same thing day after day—and we are not built for that. We are not mules. If you want to regain your energy and not be a nasty curmudgeon, you've got to do something to get out of the killer routine, *and you can't feel guilty about it*. That means booking your own office hours to read a novel in the hammock. It means calling in sick (because you are, in fact, almost dead) and lying in bed doing nothing but listening to inspiring music. I am always surprised by how energizing it is to me—and to the students—to have a sudden and unexpected break in the schedule. As an undergraduate, I learned that my most productive hours happened when I was suddenly given a gift of time free from some commitment. Think about that for a while. I know it says a lot about my INTJ-ness, but it also says something about being stretched too thin. As we all are.

Even if you are the Energizer bunny and never get burned out (no offense, but I hate you), you need to recognize that your students probably do. We normal folk get bone tired. Besides playing hooky, the single most important thing to do when the crazy days of March and April descend on us is the exact opposite of what we think we want. We think we want to phone in our teaching (and sometimes we should!), but what we really want is to open the window and let in the cold air. Now is the time to summon what you can to give a burst of energy to finish strong. Thing 10: Classroom creativity pays back in energy what it costs in content.

GET OUT OF TEACHING RUTS

Let me give you some of my favorite examples. During my second or third year of teaching, I finally learned to trust my instincts a little more on the issue of creativity in the classroom. I didn't have time to prepare the class I wanted to prepare, and my instincts were telling me that the students didn't want the same ol' same ol' anyway. Necessity is the mother of invention, so I decided to invent. Here are some things I've tried that work.

1. Set up "You teach the class" small groups. Because I teach literature by discussion and minilecture, I have never been able to do it well if I haven't read the selection recently. One morning, after staying up most of the night with a puking child, it occurred to me that the last time I had read what I assigned for the day — W. E. B. DuBois's *The Souls of Black Folk* — was five years ago. Needless to say, the puking child kept me from even cracking it open before class. So I broke the students into groups and gave them this mandate: "What is the one passage from the reading for today that you think it would be irresponsible for us not to discuss? Why? Teach that passage to the class." Win-win.

2. Assign skits in small groups. Same principle, and even more energy. I did this with first-year students once. I had assigned portions of Virginia Woolf's *A Room of One's Own*, and I really didn't feel like teaching it. I was also dead tired that day. So I broke them into groups and told them to identify the most important concept

from the reading and find some way to dramatize it. Win-win. You may be thinking, *What a waste of time.* But to you I ask, Do you really think that the students can be attentive to one more lecture on April 23? If you think that, it has been far too long since you have been a student. Look at the notes that they take in your class — if they take them at all, that is. It will be illuminating.

3. Give a "grand gesture" lecture. I owe any invention in this area to my colleague, Roger Lundin. He was known to put a trash can on his head, stand on top of the table, and do all manner of grand gestures to get the students' attention. I'll be honest: since I was always a good student, I kind of resent the dog-and-pony show approach. I've grown to despise the movie *Dead Poets Society* because it ruined teaching for the rest of us. But it is also true that grand gestures are memorable, and students love them. So in the name of my dearly departed colleague, I sometimes go for broke. For example, I teach a very difficult poem by Richard Wilbur called "Love Calls Us to the Things of This World." I think I taught this poem for three years before I knew what it meant myself. It begins with a man who wakes from sleep and thinks that angels are outside his window, when it's really just laundry. So now I string up T-shirts, climb up into a windowsill, dramatize his waking, and walk them through the poem. They laugh, look at each other awkwardly — and pay attention.

4. Read aloud. I teach literature, and often at this time of the year half the students have not done the reading. Sometimes the very best thing I can do is turn off the lights, pull out a small lamp or flashlight, and read a poem, essay, or selection from whatever we were assigned for that day. One semester I was assigned a basement classroom for my American literature class in the "spring" term. This was really a bummer until I figured out the benefits of a room that could get completely dark. So one day I killed the lights and read, by flashlight, a poem by Adrienne Rich

about the dangers of being a woman at night. You could have heard a pin drop in that room, and when students spoke up, no one could see their faces. That was something.

5. Love the students in a new way. In his poignant book *You Are What You Love*, Jamie Smith talks about how we can embody love for students in even simple ways.[5] He gives this example. He was teaching a difficult phenomenology and cognition course at 8:30 a.m., which is quite early for most students. Wanting to practice hospitality, he agreed to brew a pot of coffee for them each time the class met. (I wish I had done this when I taught Faulkner at 8:30 a.m. one year.) He found the ritual to be a wonderful way to prepare his own heart for meeting the students. There are lots of other things that can help them to feel that you know it is a tough time for them too. Bring doughnuts. Have a class in a different place (if possible). One year I invited my seven-year-old son to read a relevant children's book to my senior seminar (Mo Willems's Elephant and Piggy masterpiece, *We Are in a Book!*). That may be the only thing that some of those students will remember from the class.

6. Ask them to use a very different kind of skill. This was easy to come up with when I was teaching a course on the graphic novel. One day I asked the students to pick out a panel, page, or spread from the novel we had been assigned for the day and draw it. I brought in a box filled with random pens, crayons, pencils, and scented markers that I took from my son's room. I brought in a stack of blank paper. Then I asked the students to volunteer to show us what they drew and what they learned from it. This was so successful that I've done it many other times in different classes. When I teach Wallace Stevens, I teach the poem "Someone Puts a Pineapple Together" precisely for this reason. I put a pineapple on a stool in the

[5]James K. A. Smith, *You Are What You Love: The Spiritual Power of Habit* (Grand Rapids: Brazos, 2016).

middle of the class (with some nice music playing), and we all draw it. Then we work through the poem together. They can finally see for themselves Stevens's brilliant profusion of metaphors.

7. Rethink the last week of class. After a couple years of teaching, it becomes obvious to every educator that the last week of class before the end of each semester is a throwaway for students. They are stressed out and simply aren't going to do any of the assigned reading for your class because they are busy writing research essays for all their other classes. And everyone is tired. I teach on a M-W-F schedule, so during the last week of class I set up a graded class discussion — an idea I got from my colleague Jeff Davis. Literacy is about more than writing and reading. It is about being good listeners and deliberate speakers too. For the first step, I assign them a novel that is relatively short and easy to read. I almost always choose a graphic novel. Then, if the class is larger than fifteen students, I break them into two groups. These two groups meet with each other during class time on Monday (I only loosely supervise), during which time they plan how they want the discussion to go. I give pointers about how to organize a discussion without killing it by planning too much. Finally, one group holds their discussion on Wednesday during class time, and the other on Friday during class time. I tell them to bring snacks and make it homey. One time a student who works at a pizza place brought in two large pizzas for everyone. I have often arranged for one of these groups to do their exam in my home one evening, which is even more energizing for the students. The half of the class that is not holding the discussion gets that class day free. Relief, joy.

There are a number of other wonderful things that happen with this kind of use of the last week of class. First, I tell them that this assignment is in lieu of yet another term paper. Audible gasps of relief, joy. Second, I minimize my grading, because I evaluate their performance on the spot by listening and taking notes. Relief, joy. Third, they learn how to apply class concepts and themes to a new book, with the added test of trying to bring in the graphic novel connection, something they had not been doing all semester. Relief, joy.

8. Try the minute thesis. This is an idea I got from James Lang's book *Small Teaching*.[6] Research into the cognition of learning indicates that new learners lack the wide context and connections into which to situate what they are learning, which makes it harder for them to learn. The minute thesis can be employed at any time. Lang, an English teacher, writes on the board the last few novels the class has read. He then has them remember and write down different themes for each. He has one student come up and circle one of these themes, then draw arrows to connect to other incidences on the board. The class then has a minute to write down a connective thesis. This is a great exercise for a number of reasons. We know the material so well that we forget it is totally new to them, and they need review. They also need help making the connections that truly indicate comprehension and that put them on the road to something resembling mastery.

9. Try annotation worksheets. This is another idea I got from Lang: "Hand out a piece of paper with a section of a reading on it. Divide students into groups and ask them to annotate the hell out of it: Define keywords, identify how those words connect with other parts of the text, consider whether they point to things outside the reading. In short, dump anything they can think of onto the annotation sheet."[7] This could be used in other disciplines, too, with a bit of creativity.

[6]James M. Lang, *Small Teaching: Everyday Lessons from the Science of Learning* (San Francisco: Jossey-Bass, 2016), 106.
[7]James M. Lang, "How to Prepare for Class Without Overpreparing," *The Chronicle of Higher Education*, July 29, 2018, www.chronicle.com/article/How-to-Prepare-for -Class/244015.

10. Give some crazy, big grace. Eliminate a final assignment. Give everyone the chance to retake the test they bombed. Take a book off of your syllabus. No one will complain about having to do less. One year, after I heard a lot of whining, I gave my senior seminar the option to abandon reading Henry James's *The Wings of the Dove*. They were astonished, and then a funny thing happened. Their pride kicked in. They were not going to be defeated by Henry James. It was a wonderful moment.

11. Blow the class up. This requires a lot of advanced planning, so put a sticky note on this page and come back to it in July. My colleague Ryan Kemp, a philosophy professor, recently designed a class to respond to the reality that students have been too distracted to read outside of the classroom. He taught two sections of Existentialism that met from 6:30 a.m. to 1:05 p.m. Twenty students were enrolled in each section. The first thing he did was to collect and lock their phones away, at which many students expressed relief. 6:30 to 8:15 a.m. was spent in silent reading. After a short break, they had more time for silent reading. After brunching together (BYOBrunch), Ryan gave them a little scaffolding for future discussion, but then they read silently some more, followed by some guided in-class writing. Phones still locked up. It was only during the 11:45–1:05 portion of the class that they had more traditional discussion together based on things that came up during the morning reading, with occasional minilectures and historical material from the professor. Since the students had actually read every page, this discussion was fruitful. And get this: they read Marilynne Robinson's *Housekeeping*; Dostoevsky's *The Brothers Karamazov*; David Foster Wallace's *Infinite Jest*; and Robinson's *Home*. This class was no joke.

When I asked Ryan for some feedback about why he designed the class, he wrote, "Today's teachers have to work hard to create spaces where serious reflection and careful engagement can be reborn. For me, last semester, this meant reimagining where and how the act of reading was located and performed." The students loved it. "In my limited experience, when students are given the chance to take a course like this one, they jump at the opportunity. They have a sneaking suspicion that such a (now-quixotic) venture is precisely the reason they came to college." One student's response was typical: "I've never had a chance to sit in a book for such long periods of time so consistently before, and it really meant the books were able to change me and shape me."

I got so excited about Ryan's idea that I'm trying a new approach in my classes this year. I'm going to focus on rewarding large segments of outside-of-class CURB: Completely Uninterrupted Reading Blocks. (Is something trying to distract you? Kick it to the CURB.) The point is you don't have to use all of the dynamite to change things substantially. If you are a middle school or high school teacher who feels trapped by your day-to-day structure, then rethink it. One of my favorite teaching books of all time is by an award-winning middle school teacher, Nancie Atwell. She blew up her classroom space. There are many other ways to approach the time you have been given differently. I've listed some resources below. Allow yourself to dream big. And when you come down to the ground to work out the practicalities, think win-win.

GET OUT OF SCHOLARLY RUTS

Of course, teaching is not the only part of the scholarly life where we can get stuck and feel listless. If you are feeling that you need a resurrection in your scholarly work, try these ideas.

1. Go for a "quick success." As we all know, the academic life is full of delayed gratification. Unlike people who, say, mow lawns every day, we academics have to take our tiny morsels of satisfaction when

we can get them — which is to say, almost never. When I am really stuck in my own writing and scholarship, the best thing that I can do is to find a project that is near completion and complete it. This is true even if it takes me out of my normal routine or is involved with doing something undesirable, which is usually the case. For instance, how about revising that article that just got sent back for revision or was rejected? I have found that the comments are not usually as bad as you remember when you first read through them in despair. That's what I do, anyway. When I get feedback from manuscript reviewers, every part of me complains, "Come on! I don't need to do that! I finished that thing!" Sometimes you just need to suck it up and make the changes. You will be glad you did. Or how about plugging up the research holes on that other article that, if you were to just finish the footnotes, would be done? That kind of thing. It is difficult to overestimate the boost you can get from getting something like that out of the back of your mind.

Here's an example. One January morning I was trying to get back into my current book project, but I couldn't. My mind kept wandering to anything else for relief. Finally it occurred to me that I needed something that I could actually finish. So I opened my computer, reviewed my projects, and found one that was in the last stage of revision: an essay for a Modern Language Association volume I'm contributing to, *Approaches to Teaching Flannery O'Connor*. As English professors know, many academics in the MLA clearly have nothing better to do than nitpick the scholarship they review. The things that had stopped me from making the last-minute revisions were all psychological: I was tired of explaining myself to critics who don't understand my work, appreciate my faith commitments, and so on. But when I finally just sat down to do the task, it was far less difficult than I imagined. The payoff for doing the last step was a huge influx of energy. Much better than trying to drum up the necessary motivation to return to my book project.

2. Change your work schedule. If you've been writing Tuesday mornings, try to be more aggressive about clearing out Thursday mornings and doing it then instead. Be more diligent about planting trees with your *Forest* app, and set up accountability structures with your writing group. You can also do a grand gesture for writing too. Get a hotel room for the weekend, and power through that pile of work you just can't seem to get done. Once I cancelled my classes for the day and spent it at Starbucks doing nothing but writing letters of recommendation. It gave me a huge burst of energy to clear all that work off my to-do list.

3. Just read. Without guilt. As you will see in the next chapter, I strongly believe that reading is the most important work that scholars do. If you find yourself in a scholarly rut, sometimes the best thing to do is back off. Find a book that is related in some way, but not necessarily square on, to what you are thinking about, and let yourself read it. This is rejuvenating, and that is more important in the long run than maximizing your writing hours.

KEEP THE SABBATH WHOLLY

As I was trying to determine which month in this book to discuss the importance of Sabbath-taking, I finally settled on April because of the grind I describe above. The Sabbath was given to us as a gift, a blessed compensation for—and cessation of—labor that can feel never ending. When I think about how and why we are tempted to work constantly, I always think of the poignant line in Thoreau's *Walden*: "We do not ride on the railroad; it rides upon us."[8] Thoreau is asking readers to think about their time in a different way.

---

[8]Henry David Thoreau, *Walden and Other Writings*, ed. Brooks Atkinson (New York: Modern Library, 1992), 90.

If it costs you more of your life to earn the ticket to ride than the walk would have taken, then that was a bad trade. The railroad is no longer serving you. I encourage you to take a moment to provide your own update to Thoreau's maxim. Here are some of mine: we don't finish answering email; it finishes us. We don't grade papers; they grade us. The point is that if you never get off the train to ask questions about why you are on it to begin with, it *will* run you over. The Sabbath provides us a chance to regain perspective, to rethink how much of our lives we may be trading for not-so-great results.

There are a number of wonderful books about the meaning and importance of Sabbath rest; I've listed some of my favorites below. If I had to name the single most important spiritual decision I have made (outside of the decision to surrender my life to Christ), it would be the decision I made, years ago, to keep the Sabbath.

It started when I was an undergraduate. I don't remember what finally convinced me to try what all my unbelieving friends believed to be completely nuts: to not do any work for a twenty-four-hour period, once a week. The temptation to squeeze just a few more hours in on my reading or on that project seemed to be irresistible. I remember thinking I wouldn't be able to do it, or that my grades would suffer. But the leadership of the Christian group I was in challenged me by explaining that it was a matter of trust. Do you trust God to give you what you need in the remaining time? Or do you want to try to control the outcome of your life yourself? Do you trust God to take care of your future, regardless of the grades you may receive? I'm so glad I listened.

Today I also challenge my students, especially first-year advisees, to keep the Sabbath. I am able to do so because I can tell them truthfully that I've been keeping it since I was a first-year student at university. This means that I made it through college, high school teaching, a graduate degree, twenty years of teaching, and the writing of four books and numerous articles—all without working seven days a week. And then I tell them the truth: I made it through all of these things *because* I didn't work seven days a week. As anyone who has kept the Sabbath knows, it is a singularly restorative bliss to take your hands off of the lawnmower. Your hands have been vibrating on that mower all week, straining to keep it going. You have been pushing up hills with all your might, sweat pouring off your brow. Then suddenly you stop, take your hands off the mower, and everything falls silent. You had grown so accustomed to the clamor in your ears that you feel physical relief now that it has finally stopped. You stretch your fingers, getting the numbness out of them. You sit down. You can hear the birds, smell the newly cut grass, and rejoice in a cold glass of water. You might even pour the water over your head. This is the joy of Sabbath, and it is irreplaceable.

I am convinced that the spirit of the Sabbath is far more important than any specific directives regarding how you should keep it. I start Saturday at 5:00 p.m. and go to Sunday at 5:00 p.m. My rules are very simple: I don't do anything that feels like work to me. For instance, I might do the laundry simply because it feels good to get that out of the way, but there is no way I would answer email, grade papers, or do class prep. Though I think there are some benefits to keeping the time for spiritual things only, that actually feels like work to me. I do only the things I love that allow my soul to expand into joy—like worship. I do only the things that return me to myself as I am, not the self I think I should strive to be. I watch the Chicago Bears play. If I'm really fatigued from too much time with other people, I go to the "Church of the Holy Comforter," sit in the sun, and read things from my soul shelf. I would not give up my Sabbath rest for anything. We all need our batteries to be truly recharged. The perspective about who every day belongs to (hint: not you) is the main reward. "When the wonder of creation and our place in it are lost to us," writes Kathleen Norris, "it's often because we've lost sight of our true role as creatures—we have tried to do too much, pretending to be in such control of things that we are indispensable."[9] "The Earth is the Lord's and everything in it" (Ps 24:1). God does not need us. Instead, he allows us to participate in the work of glorifying God by living out our vocations with integrity, peace, and joy. The surprise cherry on top is the increase in productivity we enjoy when we return to work with the proper perspective.

When I was in graduate school, I carried this kind of Sabbath thinking to an even higher level than I had in the years prior to that. I discovered that trying to work all day and all evening was not helping me get things done. I found that if I worked very hard in the morning (writing), did relevant things in the afternoons (reading), and rested in the evenings (watching TV, walking), I would be more productive than I would be if I worked all the time. I always tell my students that if you work all the time, you rob yourself of what I call "shower thinking": those moments in the shower or on a walk when you weren't thinking about your project at all, and then you found the answer to the problem you had been working on. Steven Charleston puts it more poetically:

> Come stand over here, just a step or two beyond the place you have occupied for so long, where you have worn the earth smooth with your pacing, where you have spent so many hours fighting the problem you cannot seem to solve. Take a break. Catch your breath. Come stand here, where you can catch a freshening breeze and see far into the valley below. Let

---

[9]Norris, *The Quotidian Mysteries*, 26.

the distant clouds carry your worry for a while, see how the sun empties the world of shadow. The answer you seek may be just to step beyond, a higher place where the view is clear of all obstructions.[10]

When it comes to problem solving of any kind — aka thinking — there is no replacement for this kind of perspective. This is why your writing needs a "cooling off" period of at least four days before you can see it afresh. This simply cannot be rushed. Since this is the case, why not enjoy some real rest while you're at it? I remember one period during the writing of my dissertation where coming back to this one chapter felt like beating my head against the wall. I cried most of the morning and complained to my roommate in the afternoon. This went on for about a week. Finally, I just stopped looking at it and went for a long, prayerful walk. I then turned my attention elsewhere. When I returned to the chapter a few days later, I found that the problem was a lot easier to fix than I thought.

As you can see from the above paragraph, I found that I also became a much kinder person and a better roommate when I worked this way. And sure enough, I finished my PhD in five years, nowhere near the average that they kept warning us would happen with humanities PhDs. This is still how I work today, and I wouldn't change it for anything. We are not undergraduates. This career is our life, but it is not everything we are. We must not let it consume us. The only thing work-related I might do in the evening is read for classes. But this rarely happens now. I watch Netflix with my husband or read a novel I have not assigned — things I find truly relaxing. And then I wait for the promised new mercies the next day. It's the only way to live.

---

[10]Steven Charleston, quoted at PamMcDowellSaylor.com, January 2013, www.pammc dowellsaylor.com/2013/01/.

I will end this chapter with some advice I give to my students who are preparing to be high school teachers. First, God bless you. Thank you for doing this job so that I don't have to. Because this calling is more personally arduous and demands more from you, especially in terms of your waking hours, it calls for a deeper commitment to Sabbath keeping and soul care. The temptation to give more than you should to this career is intoxicating to the point of death. If you haven't seen the 2007 film *Freedom Writers*, I encourage you to do so — but not for the reasons you might think. Hilary Swank plays Ellen Gruwell, an idealistic first-year teacher at a newly integrated high school in Long Beach. Gruwell pours out her heart and soul for these students, transforming many of them from angry gangbangers into high school graduates. Her story is inspiring, and it should be. She's creative, passionate, and committed. The world needs more Ellen Gruwells. She's why we were drawn to teaching in the first place.

But that's not the whole story. Off screen Gruwell clearly has nothing left for her personal life, which subsequently falls apart. She and her husband eventually divorce, a fact that the film underplays in order to keep its idealistic vision intact. While there are no simple causes of a failed marriage, one thing is clear. There is only one of you. Furthermore, no matter how fit and fantastic you are, you cannot sprint a marathon. If you want to be able to help the next generation of students and not just the ones in front of you today, you've got to learn how to rest. You owe it to them. But most of all, you owe it to yourself.

Easter should be a time of joy, a yearly reminder that God found us to be worth dying for. It should also remind us that Christ's resurrection power is what we must learn to access in order to finish well and to flourish — not our own. If you have trouble taking your hands off of the lawnmower, then my next chapter is for you.

FOR ADDITIONAL ENCOURAGEMENT

Atwell, Nancie. *In the Middle: A Lifetime of Learning About Writing, Reading, and Adolescents.* 3rd ed. Portsmouth, NH: Heinemann, 2014.

There's a reason why this book is in its third edition. Atwell's problem-solving creativity is inspiring for everyone, not just middle school teachers. She figured out how to get even the most reluctant adolescents to read by changing the reading spaces in her classroom and the way she uses class time. In these days of Common Core foolishness, this book is essential reading.

Bass, Dorothy, and Craig Dykstra. *Teaching and Christian Practices: Reshaping Faith and Learning.* Edited by David I. Smith and James K. A. Smith. Grand Rapids: Eerdmans, 2011.

A cohort of our faculty members who were teaching advanced integrative seminars read this book together to challenge us to shake up our classrooms a bit. Smith and Smith remind readers that practices are social, communal, and inherited. They are preconscious or unconscious tools designed to inscribe a *habitus* — a way of being oriented toward the world and a particular telos. This book, written by a number of respected educators, is full of ideas about how to incorporate ancient Christian practices into a contemporary educational setting. Many of them can be redesigned for secular settings: no one will criticize you for practicing hospitality by bringing coffee for your students, for example.

Carnes, Mark C. *Minds on Fire: How Role-Immersion Games Transform College.* Cambridge, MA: Harvard University Press, 2018.

If you are interested in blowing up your classroom like I describe above, it would be a good idea to learn about the role-playing game pedagogy Carnes pioneered called Reacting to the Past. These are role-playing games designed to tap into students' natural competitiveness and curiosity, and put them in the driver's seat. Even if you don't teach history, there's a lot to learn about how to set up activities that will keep the students involved. For more information see reacting.barnard.edu.

Dawn, Marva J. *Keeping the Sabbath Wholly: Ceasing, Resting, Embracing, Feasting.* Grand Rapids: Eerdmans, 1989.

Marva Dawn's grace-saturated perspective is badly needed in the church today. This is my favorite book about why keeping the Sabbath is essential nourishment for downtrodden souls. "A great benefit of Sabbath keeping is that we learn to let God take care of us — not by becoming passive and lazy, but in the freedom of giving up our feeble attempts to be God in our own lives" (4).

Heschel, Abraham Joshua, and Susannah Heschel. *The Sabbath.* New York: Farrar, Straus and Giroux, 2005.

This book is on my soul shelf. I often retrieve it at the beginning of my sabbatical or my summer to remind myself that my spiritual goals for this time are more important than my academic goals. "Labor is a craft, but perfect rest is an art. It is the result of an accord of body, mind and imagination. To attain a degree of excellence in art, one must accept its discipline, one must adjure slothfulness" (14). The Sabbath should be the climax of living.

Lang, James M. *Small Teaching: Everyday Lessons from the Science of Learning.* San Francisco: Jossey-Bass, 2016.

Our provost, Margaret Diddams, recommended this book to our faculty, and it's a great find. Lang provides advice from cognitive research about small things teachers can do right now to make better use of the class period. Very inspiring.

May

What Momentum?
May Is for Rest

I will never forget my first year of college teaching. Since I had pretty much failed at teaching high school with any amount of joy, I worried the entire time I was earning my PhD that maybe I wasn't cut out for teaching after all. Thankfully, my fears were put to rest during that very first semester. I found that students wanted to be in my class. They wanted to be challenged to love *Walden* and Whitman as much as I did. They wanted to be inspired, and I wanted to be inspiring for them. A love fest began!

This is not to say that everything was easy. The first year of any vocation is difficult, but the difficulty of one's first year of teaching at a new place is the stuff of legends. All educators must recognize how much energy it takes to prepare new classes in order to be sure to give yourself the necessary grace whenever those new preps might happen in your career. My first year, I didn't know how to do this. By the time the spring semester ended in May, instead of enjoying a sense of accomplishment, I felt guilty about completely neglecting my scholarship. Since I also didn't know that preparation expands to fill the time you give it (Thing 1) and not to work in the evenings (Thing 2), I was completely fried. But being fried also led me to discover what is perhaps the most important thing I learned that whole year, Thing 4: Don't try to work when you are exhausted.

Moving to a new place as a single woman is difficult. But I made one close friend very quickly: Shelly. I liked Shelly immediately. Though she worked a job that was mysterious to me (computing services), she was a true kindred spirit. When she found out that I played softball, she invited me to join her team. After that long first year when I had finally dragged myself to the finish line in mid-May, I remember grilling burgers with her on my back patio on my baby Smoky Joe. I was sharing my frustration with her that I had had no time that year to work on my writing. I began to indulge in the "chunk thinking" I discussed in chapter four. In a rush I told her, "I really need to get started on a writing schedule, starting next week. I need to get moving while I still have momentum!" She laughed, looked at me with that mischievous grin I loved, and said, "What momentum?"

What momentum indeed. As the wisdom of Shelly's words sunk in, I understood that nothing good can come out of exhaustion. Sure, I could have set up a work schedule for May, forced myself to revise my dissertation, and started to look for a publisher. But the returns for my expended energy would have been poor. Consider the word *exhausted*. It comes from the Latin root *exhaust-*, which means to drain something out. It means that at one point you had something (energy), and now you don't, because it has been drained from you. In contemporary terms, you combusted all the fuel you had and sent the byproducts through the exhaust pipe. You are spent.

Of course, to learn not to work when you are exhausted requires knowing when you are exhausted and how exhausted you really are. This is not as easy as it sounds, especially for Upholders and

other perfectionists—you know who you are! The "What momentum?" question is the great gift that Shelly gave me. After I
submitted my grades, I listened to my soul. I took the rest of May
completely off, and this became my practice for many years after
that. I only changed that approach when I was able to get some
release time from teaching and could begin the summer much less
drained. I could therefore start the hard work earlier. I am so
grateful for the years I followed this practice because it enabled
me to set up real vacations during that time, at home or away,
without guilt. Guilt kills vacation time as much as exhaustion kills
productivity. It's much better to take a real break and get back in
the groove only when you are fully rested. Trust me on this one:
you won't somehow forget how to research and write. Instead, you
will begin to remember what you liked about it in the first place.

COURSE EVALUATIONS ARE LAVA

I'm no geologist, but I understand that lava is a very powerful
thing. After all, it burned Anakin Skywalker to a crisp and basically
turned him into Darth Vader. Anyone who studies lava for a living
has to learn how to respect its power. You have to learn how close
you can get to it, what instruments to use to study it, and most of
all, what kinds of information you are able to get from it.

As it is with lava, so is it with student evaluations. Because we
ask students to evaluate us at the end of the semester or year,
whatever pent-up feelings they have about us erupt onto the page
and flow on from there to burn our hearts out. Furthermore, since
their remarks are anonymous, they have no problem scorching us
with vitriol. They will take it out on us that they didn't appreciate
our tough grading standards. They will take it out on us that they
didn't like the readings. They will take it out on us (usually unwit-
tingly) that they broke up with their boyfriend or girlfriend. Even

more unfortunately, if you are a woman teaching high school or above, they will also judge you more harshly if they perceive you as a non-nurturing woman — or if they perceive you as a nurturing woman. And then, adding insult to injury, the little numbers they circle on a form are added up and used as some kind of measure of our effectiveness.

If I had a magic wand, I would use it to convince all administrators that to rely on student evaluations for promotion and advancement is a bad practice. There are all kinds of studies that show how problematic an assessment tool they are. There are also all kinds of studies that show how gender and other factors adversely affect the aggregated numbers, and how the wording of the questions always dictates the type of answers one gets.[1] But to decry these things is not my purpose here, and I have no such wand. So instead I will say, Treat those evaluations like lava! Although you could set off that volcano at the end of the semester while you are still wiped out from having given your all, I don't recommend it. Unless you enjoy being scorched. For even when the evaluations are largely positive, what you will remember — and this is basic human psychology — are the negative comments. You are in no place to hear constructive criticism at this point in the year, so what makes you think you are ready to hear unconstructive criticism? Are you a masochist?

So what are student evaluations good for, and when should you read them? This is an excellent question. In my opinion, when you are at the beginning of your career, you should only read them long after the year has cooled off, and you have the benefit of distance from your own exhaustion. You should also only read

---

[1]"Online Students Give Instructors Higher Marks If They Think Instructors Are Men." NC State News, https://news.ncsu.edu/2014/12/macnell-gender-2014/. Accessed 20 Dec. 2019. This is just one of many examples of gender bias in higher ed.

them when you are able to approach them appropriately—that is, with a massive grain of salt. In the first few years of my teaching career, the evaluations were a useful tool to help me ascertain what I needed to improve and then to make the necessary changes. But then something changed. After about five years, I already knew what I needed to improve, and hearing those things again and again and again did not help. It discouraged me instead. This was especially the case when a student's response to a question like "What did you find least effective about the course?" had a necessary inverse relationship to my particular strengths. For example, since I am good at leading discussions, I lead all my classes by discussion and minilecture. It is inevitable that some student will write (and this is, in fact, a direct quote from one of my evaluations): "I'm not paying you so that I can hear what other students have to say." This information is useless to me. Furthermore, it will not get me to change my approach, which I already know is effective, in spite of what any particular nineteen-year-old might think.

So if you want to stay inspired to teach for the long haul, I have two recommendations. The first only pertains if your evaluations are still being used by your local bean counters to determine whether or not you should receive tenure or promotion. Since I am thoroughly convinced that these assessments are mostly meaningless in determining the actual quality and effectiveness of any given teacher, I have no trouble encouraging you to play the game as best as you can. Here's how: study the language of the questions that the student evaluations ask, and then deliberately, openly, and crassly cater to it. One of our questions is something like, "How effectively did the instructor relate the subject matter to a Christian worldview?" So one semester, as an experiment, every time I was doing this type of integration, I would explicitly say something like, "And here's where we are going to see how our Christian worldview changes how we might read this text." I did nothing else differently. I always integrate my Christian worldview into teaching of literature, but this time I simply used the language on the form as often as I could. And sure enough, my scores in that area went up significantly. When filling out the form as quickly and thoughtlessly as they often do, they could not help but hear my voice in their heads saying exactly what the question was asking.

My second recommendation is this: after your first five years, don't read student evaluations unless you have to or really want to. You can also vet them through someone else, like I did for a few years with my husband's course evaluations, protecting him from the meaningless venom. Please don't misunderstand me: I am *not* saying to stop learning how to improve as a teacher. But if you want to improve, you need different kinds of information about your effectiveness, not information that can be gathered from students who are aware (or worse, unaware) of the fact that you have just bribed them with doughnuts and coffee. We should all want to improve our teaching. What you need to do is identify what specific questions your students can answer, and then ask them directly—either on paper or to their faces. Especially in new classes, near the end of the semester I will often ask my students to answer course-specific questions like the following: "What purpose do you think this particular assignment was designed to serve? Did it serve it? Why or why not?" Or, "If you could change one thing about how each class session was run, what would it be?" This kind of information is actually helpful and will not bait them to find something negative like the question "What is the least effective thing about the professor's performance?" does. The last time I checked, that particular question was still on our college-wide course evaluations, and I think it is reprehensible. We are here to teach, not to perform. Do we still ask this question? I don't know, because I haven't read my evaluations in years.

FREE-RANGE READING ON SABBATICAL

Enough of that. Let's spend the remainder of this chapter talking about something much more important: the rare and wonderful sabbatical and how to best make use of it. Again, there have been books written directly about this issue, and I am only going to speak from my own experience of having been granted two sabbaticals, for one semester each.

First, a note to high school and other teachers. Although you are not permitted sabbaticals, you still have the same need for deep, reorienting rest. Most excellent teachers I know spend their summers in professional development—earning a master's degree, writing lesson plans, reading in their fields, or doing pedagogical research. I think that every three or four summers you should completely stop that and do absolutely nothing you do not want to do for the entire summer. I call it a "Jubilee summer." Dallas Willard, the Christian philosopher of the soul, writes that "one of the greatest spiritual attainments is the capacity to do nothing."[2] If you do not take a real break from thinking about and working on your teaching, you will eventually deplete yourself to nothing. I hope the below will help to explain why.

Because educators tend to be workaholics, we tend to forget that *sabbatical* comes from the same root word as Sabbath. Everything we learned about Sabbath-taking in the last chapter applies here. Your sabbatical—or your Jubilee summer—should change you back from the scholar who has lost yourself as a person into the

---

[2]Quoted in *Sacred Ordinary Days* planner, August 13, 2017, available at www.sacred ordinarydays.com.

whole person who happens to be a scholar. It is a different relationship to time. As Abraham Joshua Heschel puts it, "There is a realm of time where the goal is not to have but to be, not to own but to give, not to control but to share, not to subdue but to be in accord."[3] Sabbaticals in many colleges have been whittled away at or even eliminated under financial pressure and the general effort to get more labor out of fewer numbers of faculty. When I was in graduate school, I thought I would get a year of paid leave for research every seven years once I got a tenured position. Instead, I discovered that I was fortunate to be at a place that paid me full time if I took off one semester, or half time if I took off the year. What's more, my institution is thinking about eliminating the one-year option altogether, which I think is a very bad idea.

Not offering and protecting a sabbatical for faculty is a big institutional mistake. Teaching is grueling work, and what is often most grueling about it is the constant effort to find and protect the chunks of time and energy that are necessary to think, write, and do meaningful research. Most of us who are college teachers became teachers because it was the only way we could get paid to think about something we really cared deeply about. We wanted to think more, not just pass on what we already know. We wanted to be lifelong learners, make contributions to our fields, and leave some kind of mark. We wanted to do these things because we know that they make us better teachers too.

My sabbaticals have been indispensable to me for precisely these reasons. Each time I have taken one, I've taken it in the spring semester because it is the hardest semester here: cold, dark, and featuring the obscenity we call February. Each fall before my sabbatical began, I prepared for it and looked forward to it, and

---

[3] Abraham Joshua Heschel and Susannah Heschel, *The Sabbath* (New York: Farrar, Straus and Giroux, 2005), 3.

each summer after, I kept working steadily as if it were part of the sabbatical. Any scholar who has had one knows how wonderful it is to finally have chunks of time to write. But by far the best thing I did on sabbatical was to rest from writing for at least half of it. In other words, I did not pressure myself to write on my proposed project until I enjoyed at least two or three months of doing nothing but reading whatever I wanted to read.

Yes, you read that correctly. The best thing I did on both sabbaticals was *not* to write all the time. Writing all the time would not serve to give me back to myself or inspire me to move forward in this career. Instead, I did something I like to call "free-range reading." Thing 8: Reading is the most vital scholarly work we do. I have come to believe that free-range reading is both absolutely necessary and woefully underemphasized for educators. I wish I could do it without guilt, because in both my sabbaticals it was the right thing to do. In both cases it led me to a far better project than I initially proposed, and it both cases it gave me supreme joy. It was the joy that got me here to begin with, rekindled.

Why? The term *free range* comes to us from the world of agriculture, and it describes the new gold standard for farming that, unsurprisingly, is actually very old. Many people today (including me) now recognize the importance of paying top dollar for beef, chicken, and pork from noncorporate farms where the animals have been allowed free-range feeding. This is because conventionally raised animals are put on grain-based diets in order to quickly increase their size before being slaughtered, and these diets significantly compromise the nutritional profile of the meat produced. Grass-fed and grass-finished beef, for example, has much higher amounts of good Omega-3 fats and much lower amounts of the bad fats than its commercially mass-produced counterpart does. Similarly, chickens that are allowed to forage for their food eat a wider range of nutrients, which makes their meat leaner and much more nutritious. This is not to mention the overuse of antibiotics and other large-farm practices that compromise our food supply.

I could go on, but I'm not here to discuss nutrition. I hope it is clear why this analogy is keen. Academics are not just teachers but thinkers and researchers. When we are herded into institutions and force-fed a scholarly diet of stuff in our disciplines in order for us to produce more — to satisfy bloated publication requirements — we are being compromised. We are being diminished from the scholars we could be into tools who produce "products" that actually hurt the health of those who consume those products. Think about it. Good, nutritious scholarly work takes time and rumination to produce. We must recognize that a couple of healthy filet mignon steaks produced by a single cow is superior to several fatty roasts that emerge from the crappy corn-fed diet of many cows. Our failure to recognize this truth has a lot of causes, not least of which is consumer capitalism and its paradigmatic lie: more is better.

Since at this point you are wondering how long I will endure comparing us to cows, I will stop with the analogy. Instead, I will share the free-range manifesto I wrote when I was on my last sabbatical. I was going to put it on the internet, but I chickened out (as it were).

FREE-RANGE READING: A MANIFESTO
FOR EXHAUSTED SCHOLARS

1. Free-range reading takes time. Institutions must prioritize it and find ways to fund it. Lack of time is the number one reason why scholars have become so narrowly focused. Even those who are predisposed toward reading widely have their desires curtailed by

committee assignments, unnecessary meetings, assessment red tape, large classes, difficulty gaining sabbatical or other release time, and bloated scholarly publication expectations. Let up on just one or two of these areas, and you will see new ideas flow — and with that, new scholarly energy. To give just one example: I teach at a liberal arts institution with a 3-3 load (teaching three classes each semester). I do not want to complain because 3-3 is *far* better than 4-4. But after twenty years of teaching, I can unequivocally say that for those who care about teaching well, a 3-3 load with upward of seventy-five students a term does not allow adequate time to think or write. To its everlasting credit, my institution blesses its faculty with the occasional opportunity to participate in advanced faith and learning seminars for which it provides four hours of release time. I have participated in three of these seminars and led one, and I can say without a doubt that my own scholarly life was saved from the despair of implosion because of the intellectual cross pollination I was able to enjoy during that time. I am truly grateful to have had these opportunities. We need to support and encourage more of this kind of thing, not less. If you are an administrator, first, God bless you for reading this. Also, please know that the investment you make in your faculty in this way will return to your institution several fold.

2. Free-range reading must be truly free. The scholar cannot be driven by "should," for what we most need to read is what we will naturally be drawn toward. We just need the fence to be opened up. Let us find the pasture! Once we can get away from the expected diet, we can find the food that truly nourishes us. It will be surprising what we will discover and become. The theologian might read a Philip Pullman novel and find a new way to understand and articulate why theology is crucial. The historian might find stunning new insights into Napoleon's mindset by reading

contemporary neuropsychology. The physicist may be drawn to Robert Bly to find words for what he has learned about consciousness. The literary scholar may discover that reading Karl Popper opens up the world of fiction in a way she never imagined. When I was an undergraduate student, I was stunned to discover that Virginia Woolf's father had told her not to worry about reading what she thinks she "should" because there were plenty more things worth reading than she could possibly get to in a lifetime. She took his advice.

3. Free-range reading cannot be measured. I'm writing these words during my second sabbatical so that I can remember how glad I was that I had the courage to do it during my first one. I read every day, whatever I wanted to and wherever I wanted to, without forcing myself to write. It was amazing—like sitting down to a sushi dinner after eating rubber banquet chicken for seven years. I waited until that summer to begin to write, and I was able to finish my second book over the following five years, writing primarily during the summers. Could I have written a book in two years without all of this free-range reading? Yes. But it would not have been—could not have been—that book. I can't be the judge of the impact on others of this specific scholarly project, but the impact on me and my own thinking and my own teaching was tremendous. The problem is that this kind of impact by definition cannot be quantified. This is why I hate the culture of assessment so much. It mistrusts scholars, treats us like infants, claims that more is better, and bean-counts us all into an early grave. Our creativity is being prematurely killed. With our creativity goes our very souls. With our souls go the souls of those who end up in our classes, trying to drink from a dry spigot.

This manifesto is meant to be a little extreme; it's a manifesto. I wrote it for myself because I knew it was not helpful to feel guilty about the fact that I was spending three weeks reading Hans Urs von Balthasar's massive theological aesthetics, *The Glory of the Lord*. As I reflected on my guilt, I recognized that it did not come from inside influences but from outside ones: I've been given a sabbatical, so I should be churning out a lot of stuff now! But this kind of pressure is not productive and cannot be. We need to encourage one another that time spent in free-range reading and full-on rest is not wasted, frivolous, or unproductive. When I am spending my days deep in study without anxiety about producing, I think about the work that Thoreau did at Walden pond: the work of living and observing. He kept journals that he later wrote from, condensing two years into one. By now you will have discovered that *Walden* is one of my favorite books, and lines from it reverberate in my soul. Reflecting on the many days he spent neither reading nor working, he writes,

> Sometimes, in a summer morning, having taken my accustomed bath, I sat in my sunny doorway from sunrise till noon, rapt in a revery, amidst the pines and hickories and sumachs, in undisturbed solitude and stillness, while the birds sing around or flitted noiseless through the house, until by the sun falling in at my west window, or the noise of some traveller's wagon on the distant highway, I was reminded of the lapse of time. I grew in those seasons like corn in the night, and they were far better than any work of the hands would have been.[4]

I have thought of my own intellectual and spiritual life, which are indissolubly connected, exactly this way many times. "I grew in those seasons like corn in the night." All we have to do is allow ourselves to be planted. Growth happens when we sleep too. And it is all by God's hand.

---

[4]Henry David Thoreau, *Walden and Other Writings*, ed. Brooks Atkinson (New York: Modern Library, 1992), 108-9.

I think it is foolish to forget that a scholar's life most often works this way—quietly and invisibly. It is not what gets thrown on Twitter and blogs that defines us but what we discover when we dig deep into the intellectual ground that God has given us to till. Although A. G. Sertillanges, author of the 1934 classic *The Intellectual Life*, doesn't seem to think that women can be intellectuals, I still cherish his conviction that the scholarly life is one of disciplined, patient, and humble attention to a problem we are trying to solve. "The jingling bells of publicity tempt only frivolous minds," he writes. He continues,

Ambition offends eternal truth by subordinating truth to itself. Is it not a sacrilege to play with the questions that dominate life and death, with mysterious nature, with God—to achieve some literary or philosophical celebrity at the expense of the true and independently of the true? Such aims, and especially the first mentioned, would not sustain the seeker; his effort would speedily be seen to slacken, his vanity to fall back on some empty satisfaction, with no care for the reality of things.[5]

Sertillanges was writing this before the temptation to internet fame. Today it is easier than ever to get quick publicity for shoddy work. While it is important to cultivate different audiences as a part of our vocation, I despise the idea that we should work by throwing things at the wall and seeing what sticks. Sertillanges's view of truth might be a bit naive and elitist, but his view of what our aim should be is not. We should be concerned with ultimate reality—however that might be discerned through our individual disciplines—and that takes time, humility, and disciplined attention. We grow like corn in the night.

---

[5] A. G. Sertillanges, OP, and James V. Schall, SJ, *The Intellectual Life: Its Spirit, Conditions, Methods*, trans. Mary Ryan (Washington, DC: The Catholic University of America Press, 1992), 6.

Because intellectual growth and productivity cannot be easily measured, I believe we need to rethink the way sabbaticals are granted at the institutional level. Sabbaticals should not be limited to those who can produce at breakneck speed, but should be granted to any devoted teacher who simply wants to read more, learn more, or be challenged by some new area in or around his or her field. That this kind of sabbatical cannot be prioritized for funding by the powers at large is difficult for me to understand. I agree that we do not want to reward pedestrian educators who have no discernible intellectual life. The potential for abuse should be addressed. But for the one scholar who abuses his or her sabbatical, there are thirty or more who have been rendered unable to enjoy it by the expectations of product. And so they go dutifully to the trough instead of joyfully out to pasture. They go to the trough with guilt, stress, anxiety, and, above all, the self-defeating, self-flagellating whip that strikes "Write, write, write—or you don't deserve this time at all."

You have heard that negative voice inside your head. Instead, I tell you, "It's May. Go out and enjoy the pasture while the sun is shining."

FOR ADDITIONAL ENCOURAGEMENT

Someone, I. M. *That Book You've Been Dying to Read.*

It could be a novel. It might be a cookbook. The summer that I spent revising this book I also read a memoir, a Chinese sci-fi novel, a feminist sci-fi novel, a brilliant collection of short stories by a new writer, two books about middle age, and some more Brené Brown. And that's not all. Find your own pasture.

June

Get to Work: Aggressively Protect Your Summer

O ne of the funniest things I've ever read about how hard
it is to write comes from Flannery O'Connor. O'Connor had
lupus in the 1960s, when it was far less manageable. She was on
her deathbed when she finished what would be one of the most
significant stories of her short but brilliant career, "Parker's Back."
Because of her illness, she had never been able to do a lot of
writing, and near the end of her life, her productivity window was
reduced to about two hours a day. In a letter she wrote, "I asked
the doctor if I could sit up at the electric typewriter and work. You
can work, says he, but you can't exert yourself. I haven't quite
figured this out yet; anyway I am confined to these two rooms and
the porch so far and ain't allowed to wash the dishes. I guess that
is exerting yourself where writing is officially not."[1]

O'Connor knew that her one thing was to be a writer, and the
world is a much better place for her determined focus. She also
knew that writing of any sort is extremely hard work. Since she was
ill, she fiercely protected her energy so that she could focus on
story writing. She used her morning hours to labor over the

---

[1]Flannery O'Connor, *Collected Works* (New York: Library of America, 1988), 1212.

writing, received visitors in the afternoon on her porch, and rested and slept in the evening.

I don't have a debilitating disease, but an approach similar to O'Connor's is still the only way I've ever found I can write. Any time after 2:00 p.m. in the afternoon, the amount of energy I put in is not commensurate with the product I churn out. But if I put myself in front of the computer from 6:00 a.m. until 1:00 p.m., Monday through Friday, I can get an awful lot done. I remember the day in graduate school when I began to notice an unwavering pattern. When I was making the really great discoveries and my fingers couldn't keep up with my brain, I would glance at the clock, and it would be somewhere between 9:00 and 11:00 a.m. Every time.[2]

It is worth returning to the key points I made in chapters two and three. First, locate the most important project. Then find the one thing you need to do to advance that project. Finally, remove all distractions and plant that forest. If Richard Koch is correct that 20 percent of the work you do achieves 80 percent of the results, you need to find a way to give at least two or three hours of your day to your research and writing and really drill down.[3] So for most of us, the first one thing you need to do is to protect your summer alone time. Aggressively.

A. G. Sertillanges's book *The Intellectual Life* has some great reminders to scholars that our work is fundamentally different from that of others because it requires this kind of solitude—and lots of it. My husband probably regrets handing me this book because I've got these words on the door of my study now:

---

[2]What my husband discovered early in our relationship is also true: when I get sleepy or declare I am going to bed, it is almost always 10:17 p.m.

[3]Gary Keller and Jay Papasan, *The ONE Thing: The Surprisingly Simple Truth Behind Extraordinary Results* (Austin: Bard, 2013), 37.

You must defend your solitude with a fierceness that makes no distinctions whatever. If you have duties, satisfy their demands at the normal time; if you have friends, arrange suitable meetings; if unwanted visitors come to disturb you, graciously shut the door on them.

It is important, during the hours sacred to work, not only that you should not be disturbed, but that you should know you will not be disturbed; let perfect security on that score protect you, so that you can apply yourself intensely and fruitfully. You cannot take too many precautions about this. Keep a Cerberus at your door. Every demand on you from outside is a loss of inner power and may cost your mind some precious discovery: 'when half-gods go, the gods arrive.'[4]

I don't know what Cerberus has to do with it, because knowing that I will not be disturbed is my land of Canaan (unfortunately it is usually more like Shangri-La). Sertillanges points out that you can work at the same time with others as long as they are quiet in the same way, because their focus can fuel yours. But that solitude must be defended like a fortress. "You must listen to no one, neither indiscreet friends, nor ununderstanding relatives, nor chance comers, nor charity itself. You cannot be charitable in every direction at once. You belong to truth; serve her first."[5] This may sound lofty, but it motivates me. I am doing what I was called to do. Since I have a lot of "ununderstanding relatives," I know just how difficult it can be to arrange for and protect this time. It takes a certain amount of trust that what you will be able to produce down the road will be a gift for others. That is not always easy to

---

[4]A. G. Sertillanges, OP, and James V. Schall, SJ, *The Intellectual Life: Its Spirit, Conditions, Methods*, trans. Mary Ryan (Washington, DC: The Catholic University of America Press, 1992), 98.
[5]Sertillanges and Schall, *Intellectual Life*, 99.

believe in because it requires believing that you have been called to do this work and that God is working through it.

I know that some of us have chosen this career because we get the summers "off," and we want to use the sunny weeks to enjoy long vacations and extended time with family. If that's the case, that's fine; just recognize that there's a substantial "coasting cost" in terms of career advancement and other perks of the profession. Most of us do not have that problem. We want to write, but we have children who are home from school or obligations to summer abroad programs, or feel pressed to moonlight to supplement a feeble income.

Beyond what I already covered in chapter five, I do not have near enough space in this book to address the question of how many children you choose to have, how you work out domestic responsibilities with your spouse, and so on. These are issues that you need to spend some actual time thinking through, not just settling them by default. I know how tempting it is to take the default position. We do not call ourselves "the last-minute Lakes" for nothing. We are always the last ones turning in stuff, signing up for stuff, or what have you. We've paid the price for this failure to plan over and over again.

Since I already mentioned the deception of work-life balance, here I want to make a different point. As academics, it is important to avoid the common trap of undervaluing our own "free" time, especially in the summer. With strategic planning, a commitment that our time is worth it, and a focused work schedule, we can find a way to plan for our children so that we have some time to write. Admittedly, my husband and I have only one child, so our situation is different from that of many other academic families. But it still raises significant challenges. Even if neither one of us were working during the summer, we would not be able to find enough things for our son to do to keep him from pestering us, nonstop, to let him rot his brain out on video games. We discovered early on that our local park district's summer camp costs a little over $1,100 for him to attend five days a week, all summer. This money can also be saved, tax free, in my flexible benefit account. Many academics make the strategic mistake of thinking $1,100 not spent on this camp is $1,100 saved, but in this case, it most definitely is not.

Consider this example. I enjoy reading and writing for Christian publications like *Books & Culture* (alas, no more!) and *The Cresset*. It keeps my writing from being overly academic and gives me a different kind of audience that I desire to cultivate. It also happens to be true that if I can make even a little bit of extra cash for these short articles I publish, I can pay for the whole summer of my son's camp pretty quickly. Some of you may be thinking, *True for you, but the articles I write don't pay, and I won't make one red cent off of my academic books*. On the contrary, I argue (I love Aquinas) whether that is really true. If your scholarly book helps you to get a promotion, have you not gotten paid for it? If publications have led you to be invited to give keynote addresses, have you not gotten paid for that time again? To save money by not sending your child to day camp is penny wise but pound foolish. If you have three children, you can usually afford for all three children to attend camp together for two or three days a week for the entire summer (or every day for a portion of it). At my son's camp last summer, they did crafts, took field trips, and swam three days a week. He had much more fun than he would have had with his boring mom, and I finished one book and started another—the one in your hands right now.

Please do not misunderstand me. If you chose this career for its flexibility in allowing you to have more time with your children, particularly during the summer, then that's wonderful! I personally cannot be that mom. As our son aged out of day camp, we had to work harder to piece together things he was willing to do during the day. That was challenging, but it was still far better for us than having him mope around at home. Our area churches are full of recent college graduates with boundless love and energy to give, and they give it liberally to summer programs like VBS. Local high schools have youth sports camps, as does our college. We also live near a community college that offers youth academy programs like Lego robotics and other STEM classes. But if you make the choice to stay at home with your children all summer, you need to recognize that it is a choice you made. You cannot expect from yourself the same amount of productivity that you would have had if you had blocks of time to sit in front of your computer and write. And that is just fine. Own your choice, and enjoy it.

I want to use this same logic to consider the tricky issue of teaching in summer programs. Wheaton has a number of faculty-led summer programs, and our department has one of the most intensive of them: Wheaton in England. The program is excellent for student recruitment to our major, as it builds an irreplaceable *esprit de corps* among students and faculty alike. When I applied for the job, it sounded like something I really wanted to do, especially as a poor graduate student who had never been to England. But when I started teaching, I quickly learned that this particular program wasn't just a few weeks in the summer. It was eight weeks of teaching in addition to the whole prior year spent planning and doing other administrative work for it. This means making phone calls, rescheduling reservations, planning excursions, and so on. If this is the case for your summer program, I cannot recommend that anyone who has significant scholarly goals agree to participate. It is simply not worth it. Again, please don't misunderstand me. If you want to teach in your department's summer abroad program, then do it. But unless it is a part of your contract, don't go because you are an Obliger or an Upholder. Don't go for the additional income, which is not commensurate with the load for most programs. Go because it is something you want to do, and go with joy.

I'm also aware that great disparities in summer program expectations exist in my college and in others. Small foreign language programs are especially burdened, both because language study requires work abroad, and the departments tend to be smaller. If you agree to take a job as a foreign language professor, make sure you are aware of the stated demands and hidden expectations and are on board with all of them. If you find yourself in a situation in which you are expected to teach abroad every other summer or more often, then you have to adjust your own approach to scholarly work accordingly. Fellow faculty members and administrators also need to understand that such faculty members cannot have the same productivity demands placed on them for promotion and tenure. That is the height of unfairness, and it is biting the hand that feeds the students the most.

FORM YOUR OWN DANG WRITING GROUP

Like a lot of new faculty members at Wheaton, when I arrived, I expected a different kind of community life than what I found. I thought my colleagues in and outside of my department would want to meet to discuss scholarly things or to just hang out. I soon discovered that almost everyone, in addition to being highly introverted, was stretched so thin that even simple social events did not happen with much regularity. The social gatherings that did happen, like the obligatory department Christmas party, felt forced and unnatural. Other gatherings, long extant, were closed to me.

Now that I'm a senior faculty member, I want to be fair to the people who were senior to me by acknowledging my own failures in this area. Once you start a family, get conscripted into committees, and begin to have more church responsibilities, squeezing in time for collegial gatherings is difficult. It didn't help that initially our faculty members were constrained (at that time) by signing a pledge that we would not consume alcoholic beverages. A cold pint of Lagunitas can go a long way toward promoting a warmer collegiality, which we have now been permitted to rediscover.

For a number of years, I grumbled about my social situation. I felt as hurt as a thirteen-year-old unfriended on social media. It was substantially worse when I discovered that a few different groups of male colleagues had been gathering together with a fair amount of regularity, and, for whatever reason, I was not invited. As a faculty member, particularly someone with wide interdisciplinary interests, it is a blow to the ego to feel that no one wants to share ideas with you. After a few years of unsuccessful attempts to find a way into what I perceived to be the "in" crowd, my response became a spiritual problem for me. I began to be angry, withdraw emotionally from my own department, and build my social and intellectual life almost entirely outside of Wheaton. I went to my office to teach, to grade, and to meet students, and that was it.

Like any self-protection mechanism, this response had its good side. It was very helpful to me to focus on my work while I was in my office so that I didn't have to take it home with me. And as I've written in this book, I still generally believe in that approach. But it is also true that while I'm never going to be the kind of colleague who has my door open all the time, I don't want to be the kind of colleague whose door is closed all of the time either. As my son got older and I could do more things, I really longed for more intentional, scholarly community.

It was only when I was reading Gretchen Rubin's book *The Happiness Project* that it suddenly occurred to me: stop waiting around to be invited into the elite cabal, and *form my own dang group!* Rubin has a chapter on the benefits of working groups, and I knew instantly that it was exactly what I needed. As I journaled about it, three female colleagues immediately came into mind. I invited them to meet at the source of the world's greatest chicken fingers, the Village Tavern of Carol Stream. I soon discovered that they were all on board, and they were as excited as I was. We are now VTS: the Village Tavern Scholars and Scribes.

I'm amazed that it took me this long to come up with an idea that has been the single most productive move of my academic career. The four of us meet for breakfast about once a month, primarily to check in on each other's goals and progress on writing projects. But of course we have also become closer friends. We laugh about our husbands and children (we have ten children among the four of us) in order to keep from crying. We meet at the Tavern for chicken fingers and cocktails to celebrate book contracts and finished projects, or just because sometimes we really need chicken fingers, loaded potato skins, a pint of Guinness, and each other. Although we often do send work around to each other to read and get feedback, that is actually not the group's primary purpose. Our primary purpose is to provide loving accountability and encouragement because that is what we all need the most. We have discovered and rediscovered together the truth of Jesus's words, "Again, truly I tell you, if two of you agree on earth about anything you ask, it will be done for you by my Father in heaven. For where two or three are gathered in my name, I am there among them" (Mt 18:19-20). Writing and teaching can be very lonely work.

It is helpful to see that others struggle with the same things that we do. We get writing blocks. We get confused about what to write next, get rejected by publishers, and get worn out—sometimes for months on end. We have learned to listen to each other when we say, "You have three children at home! This amount of work is the best you can do right now. *And that is completely okay.*"

Of all of the things I have done with colleagues, forming this writing group has had the single biggest positive impact on my work and my sanity. Form your own dang writing group! You will be very glad you did. But you can't have BAJ, Kind Eyes, and Hot Cross for your group. They are in mine.

FOCUS ON QUALITY

The last issue I want to address in this chapter is perhaps the most complex of all: how your work as a teacher and a scholar is received. There is a great deal of performance anxiety among junior faculty members at Wheaton. Since I've never taught at any other college, I don't know if our anxiety levels are higher here than they are elsewhere, but I suspect they are. Regardless of campus culture, most junior faculty members have at least three audiences on their minds all the time: the college (administration and fellow faculty), the students, and their larger guilds. And, wouldn't you know it, they all seem to want different things, especially for a teacher at a Christian college.

I have only ever done one thing when it comes to trying to satisfy all three audiences, and that is this: I don't try. As a largely apolitical-INTJ-perfectionist-Questioner-Reformer (number 1 on the Enneagram), all my motivation to excel comes from within, and I tend to be my own toughest critic. I don't care much what others think if I believe I'm doing the best that I can do. So of course I think that is the approach everyone should take.

But I also recognize that this is easier said than done, especially for Obligers and Upholders. It is true that tenure and professional advancement, our very livelihood, is at stake. This is why we must surround ourselves with trusted friends who can help us be true to ourselves, to help us to grow into the best teachers and scholars *we* can be. Because if you try to be everything to everyone, you will fail. The Obligers I know may understand this, but it is clear that they have not internalized it. If I knew how to help my insecure faculty friends with this, I would, because it is too great a burden for anyone to carry.

Perhaps a thought experiment is in order. I use this experiment to help students to think about their participation in my classes. Imagine that you are a field goal kicker on a professional football team, and you are called upon in the last second of a game to make the winning kick. Since most of us are not field goal kickers, we have to try to imagine the pressure and terror of your job being literally on the line. What is the one sure-fire way of missing the kick? Assuming that you have practiced kicking field goals and are still learning and improving your method, the only sure-fire way of missing the kick is to worry about missing it. The way to make it is to step up and do it as unselfconsciously as possible, automatically, out of the place of your training, with a singular focus on one thing: the kick itself. Likewise, being self-conscious about how others receive your academic work or your teaching is the quickest way to fail. Once you've learned the methods that work best for you, you've got to trust your training and let go. You have to know ahead of time that sometimes you will miss, but that's okay. Pick yourself up, make the necessary adjustments for the next semester or scholarly article, and try again.

I know that this is easier said than done. Impostor's syndrome is real. I remember sitting in literary conferences, especially early in my career, thinking that I was the only one who couldn't follow this paper, that I was the only one who didn't speak Lacan, that I was the only one who felt like a six-year-old child who had wandered into a calculus class by mistake. Imposter syndrome rears its ugly head especially when a paper or book manuscript gets rejected. But while it is real, impostor's syndrome is also inaccurate. Everyone has felt it at one point or another, and those who haven't felt it are probably so arrogant that they don't recognize it. Although arrogant superstars are the worst possible models for Christian scholars and teachers, we still stupidly envy them.

Something I am still learning is that the only way to handle impostor's syndrome is to call it out and then ignore it. God did not put you here by accident. Your education degree or your PhD was not an accident. Self-assurance is not arrogance; it comes from being confident that God doesn't make mistakes. If you find you cannot ignore impostor's syndrome, then we need to talk about shame and envy. Shame seduced envy. They had an illegitimate child: impostor's syndrome. Brené Brown is a shame researcher who has written many encouraging books about how debilitating shame can be. While guilt can be a positive emotion that says, "You should have spent last week writing a little bit every day; change that behavior next week," shame is always negative because it says, "You obviously can't write anything worth reading, so why bother?" Shame, which stays hidden, seduces envy from the shadows. It's an easy conquest because if we feel worthless inside, we look at everyone else's success with an aching, corrosive longing. I've always cherished the wisdom of Proverbs on this: "A heart at peace gives life to the body, but envy rots the bones" (Prov 14:30 NIV). Proverbs contrasts a heart at peace with envy, instructing us that the only way to counter envy is to know who you are in Christ Jesus.

I admit that I have felt very strong envy before. I have said some pretty bad things about scholars my age or younger who seem so quickly and easily to gain the larger audience that I want but cannot seem to find. These scholars write about the same issues I've been thinking and writing about for years, but they have gained the lucrative speaking engagements, they sell more than a few copies of books, and their names are known. Even as I write these words now, I can feel my bones rotting. The only thing that helps me is to remember that God gave me my own gifts and a clear calling. It is not up to me to manufacture the outcome of my faithfulness.

When I started teaching at Wheaton, there were a few very strong teachers who all the students practically worshiped. The Legends. I'm sure you have a few of them at your school too. I thank the Lord that I learned early on that if I tried to imitate them, I would become a miserable, second-rate version of myself. God gave them the gifting to be the quarterbacks with the dazzling plays. God gifted me, instead, to be the middle linebacker who inspires the team to fight. I chose this football metaphor deliberately, because one of my favorite quotations of all time comes from the accomplished Baltimore Ravens linebacker Ray Lewis: "Success is one thing; impact is another." I have a choice. I can rot with envy that I am not the star quarterback, or I can perfect my game and remember that my contribution is important. It should be no surprise that this solution to envy is thoroughly scriptural:

> For the body does not consist of one member but of many. If the foot should say, "Because I am not a hand, I do not belong to the body," that would not make it any less a part of the body. And if the ear should say, "Because I am not an eye, I do not belong to the body," that would not make it any less a part of the body. If the whole body were an eye, where would be the sense of hearing? If the whole body were an ear, where would

be the sense of smell? But as it is, God arranged the members in the body, each one of them, as he chose. If all were a single member, where would the body be? As it is, there are many parts, yet one body. (1 Cor 12:14-20)

As with spiritual gifts, so is it with our vocations. We are only responsible for being faithful in exercising the particular gifts that God has given each one of us.

LET GO OF RESULTS

What I am saying applies to teaching as well as scholarship: let go of results. The surest way to fail as a teacher is to care too much about what your students think of you. Stay busy caring for them out of the core of who you are, and the rest will follow. If you are at a liberal arts college or at a high school, the students are your primary audience. Do not be ashamed to focus on them to the exclusion of someone else's goal for what it means to be a productive scholar. Find out what your college requires for tenure and advancement, then set up a schedule that will enable you to meet those goals. There is nothing wrong with being a journeyman academic who positions yourself primarily as a teacher and mentor. There is also nothing wrong with being a journeyman academic and discovering you have administrative gifts and pouring yourself into that service. The first nineteen years I taught at Wheaton, I was blessed to have a department chair who recognized those gifts in herself and gave them indefatigably day after day. And by the way, if you are working with someone who does this kind of service, you must never forget that it is his or her sacrifice that makes your work possible. He or she is a quiet hand so that you can be a loud-mouth. We cannot all do everything, so let us stop criticizing the very people who make it possible for us to do more of what we are called to do.

If you are interested in impacting your guild and the larger public beyond, things can be tricky, especially at a Christian college. In literary studies, the larger guild often actively rejects the integrated approach that my college and students most want from me.[6] The best way out of this quandary is to find a niche and work your way into it the best you can. I have always been grateful that I am primarily known as a Flannery O'Connor scholar, because the larger guild in O'Connor studies tends to be composed of Christians from institutions all over the world. We are a loving group. Since I've never been good at networking, it was fun to find myself being invited to speaking engagements with the same group of people who slowly became good friends and allies. The work I've done on O'Connor has become a home base for me to expand into other areas with much more confidence. I'm moving into Cormac McCarthy studies, a discourse community that shares some of the same scholars, though most of the folks there are new to me.

Regardless of your discipline, the quality of your teaching and your writing should always be your primary concern. I have generally believed that with patience and persistence, the cream will rise to the top — even in the largest and scummiest of milk barrels. Some of the best advice I received about publishing came from Susan Felch, who told me early in my career that what separates published writers from unpublished ones is envelopes and stamps.

---

[6]It was, after all, an English professor from the University of Pennsylvania who publicly argued that Christian colleges should not be accredited because we actually expect faculty members to believe in crazy things. "Consider those Christian colleges that require their faculty members to sign a 'faith statement' consenting to such scientifically preposterous propositions as, for example, that God created Adam and Eve, who were real historical figures and who are the actual ancestors of all humanity. Other religious institutions avoid such flamboyantly explicit demands on the faculty, but many of them draw lines around what is regarded as acceptable teaching and research. And yet those intellectually compromised institutions routinely receive accreditation from their regional commissions." Peter Conn, "The Great Accreditation Farce," *The Chronicle of Higher Education*, June 30, 2014, www.chronicle.com/article/The-Great -Accreditation-Farce/147425.

Alas, "email attachments" doesn't have the same ring, but the advice is the same. Even so, we need to acknowledge that twenty-first century publishing realities are very different than twentieth-century ones. Although the ramifications of those differences are outside of the scope of this book, I want to point out that no scholar today can afford not to think about how blogs, Twitter, online journals, digital media, and other publishing explosions factor in to your future. It is easy to feel very old very fast. The trick is not to become a curmudgeon and not to give up.

From where I sit, it seems to be the case that for any of our work to get noticed by our guilds or a larger audience, regardless of the venue, you must be at least two of the following five things:

1. Lucky

2. Really good at what you do

3. Relevant

4. Well-positioned already

5. Full of grit

One of these five is not enough to cut it. Assuming that you are hoping to be well positioned, and knowing that you cannot control luck, you are left with three things you must strive for: to be really good at what you do, relevant, and/or full of grit. For some people, the idea of being a relevant scholar is already an oxymoron, but I'm not necessarily talking about general-audience relevance. You can do relevant work within your own discipline, an interdisciplinary niche, or the church at large. A very fine example of the latter is the scholarship of my friend and colleague Bill Struthers. A neuroscientist, Bill researches how pornography affects the brain. His book, *Wired for Intimacy*, has impacted the conversation within the church on an extremely important topic. Others in his guild may ignore his research, but it doesn't matter; Bill knows this work is needed, and he gets invited all over the world to talk about it.

I envy Bill for the type of research he does, because the relevance as well as the measure for being really good at what you do (as he is) are crystal clear. It is not so clear for other disciplines. But with a little focused thinking, you can and should discover it for yourself and your students. Stephen J. Aguilar makes an excellent case that everyone in the academy should be intentional in their efforts to establish a scholarly identity. "Put simply, your scholarly identity is the product of your training, areas of expertise, methodological inclination, interests, publications, research agenda, reputation and anything else that may be important in your field." According to Aguilar, this is important for the moment when someone, somewhere asks the question, "You know who would be good for this? [Insert scholar.]"[7] The goal is to have your name be the one the people you care about put in the brackets when they ask this question.

Thinking about my scholarly identity over the years has clarified my vocational choices as the right ones for me. I have always believed that being a literary scholar means helping people to understand why we must read imaginative work, and not just nonfiction. Everything I do revolves around persuading others of the relevance of fiction to their lives. Everything I do comes out of a deep conviction that there is a certain kind of thinking that we can only do through literature and not anywhere else.

Am I good at it? Have I made an impact? I hope so. But thankfully, that is not for me to determine. After you have done the best you can do, at some point you simply have to decide to lean into your vocation and leave the results to God.

---

[7]Stephen J. Aguilar, "Establishing Your Scholarly Identity," *Inside Higher Ed*, July 26, 2018, www.insidehighered.com/advice/2018/07/26/shaping-scholarly-identity-helps-you-do-what-you-want-academe-opinion.

FOR ADDITIONAL ENCOURAGEMENT

Burge, Gary M. *Mapping Your Academic Career: Charting the Course of a Professor's Life.* Downers Grove, IL: IVP Academic, 2015.

This book is a helpful guide for professors in each of three developmental stages in one's career, which Burge identifies by the approximate age a professor usually is when he or she hits that stage: 28-38; 34-55; 50-70. A professor in the first stage is searching for security; the second, success; the third, significance. Burge gives solid advice and admonition gleaned from his many years as an effective scholar and teacher.

Lamott, Anne. *Bird by Bird: Some Instructions on Writing and Life.* New York: Anchor, 1995.

Every serious writer I have ever met has read and benefitted from this hilariously encouraging book. If my readers think I have even half her insight and grace, I will be delighted. It is a good read for advanced students too.

Silvia, Paul J. *How to Write a Lot: A Practical Guide to Productive Academic Writing.* Washington, DC: American Psychological Association, 2007.

A number of my colleagues — notably, not just in the humanities — have found this to be an instructive and inspiring little book. If you are looking for some strategies you can implement today to help you get your projects done, this book is for you.

12

July

Bug Bites and Broken Teeth

O ne lovely day in early July, I was happy and relaxed, having dinner with my close friend and writing group colleague, Kind Eyes. Although Kind Eyes has four children of her own and I have only one, she does a better job than me of getting out of the house. Still, neither one of us does it enough, and we know it. We had just received our enormously decadent meals—and declared we should do this more often—when I bit into my bison burger and heard the crunch that someone with dental problems never wants to hear. I had broken one of my crowns. Again. I have so many crowns it seems I've robbed the British museum. I make jokes with my dentist about setting up a tent in her office. The crown that broke happened to be the one attached to one of my two dental implants. This particular implant was the one that had replaced a failed molar—a tooth that had to be pulled only after it had had a root canal and a previous crown of its own. We are talking about thousands of after-insurance dollars, all for one tooth.

The next day when I called my dentist, I admit it: I was grumbling. Earlier in the week I had taken my son fishing at the pond that is a short walk from our house. He wisely went home before dusk, while I stayed, trying to snag those elusive smallmouth bass I know are in there. I didn't catch any bass, but I got so chewed up by bugs that my skin was bruised with some sort of allergic reaction. I have never experienced anything like this. I had three different types of anti-itch cream, but I still had to sit in an oatmeal bath to get any relief. When I wasn't in the bath, I had to ice the bites. It took over a week for my body to stop itching. I was an itchy mess while I was on the way to the dentist, and I began to feel very angry.

And then it occurred to me, thankfully sooner rather than later: *This is just bug bites and broken teeth.* Minor inconveniences, easily endured. Truly light and momentary troubles. I felt thoroughly chastened when I thought about the much more intense struggles of family members and colleagues: cancer, deaths in the family, struggles with deep depression, unemployment. When I was sixteen, I was at fault in a very bad automobile accident. Neither party was hurt—I was driving a rusty but indestructible 1972 Chevy station wagon that my father had dubbed "The Silver Bullet"—but the other person's Camaro was totaled. I was devastated by guilt and shame. I was struggling to process the whole mess when my best friend's mother told me, "It's just heaps of metal on the road. That's all it is. Just heaps of metal." Since then I have tried to apply this wisdom everywhere. A broken tooth? It's just money. And thankfully I have dental insurance. I am one of the most blessed people in the world because I can afford to have an implant. Furthermore, I live in a time in history when it is possible to have root canals, implants, and all other kinds of quality dental work, all under adequate local anesthetic. Read any text from the nineteenth century that mentions dental care, and you will surge with gratitude.

While it has become a platitude doled out by Oprah, it is still true. If we want to inhabit our lives with joy, we must cultivate an attitude of gratitude. In this chapter I would like to share the little bit of what I have learned about how to grow in the kind of joy our students can inhabit along with us.

RECEIVE GRACE, ACHIEVE GRATITUDE

Most of what I know about cultivating gratitude I have picked up from Andre Dubus, a Catholic writer I routinely teach in my contemporary American literature class. Dubus was a reluctant Marine who was born to be a writer. He looks like Hemingway and writes with the same discipline. His stories depict characters in intense dilemmas that prove the quality of their inner character. One well-known example is "A Father's Story," in which a devout Catholic man has to decide what to do after his daughter accidentally hits and kills a hiker on the side of the road and drives away in fear. Like some of my favorite writers about spiritual disciplines, Dubus has always understood that a "What Would Jesus Do?" bracelet will not help in these situations. When speared by the horns of a dilemma, only the prior spiritual training you have undergone will help you make the right decision.

Dubus had already written many such stories when he faced an even bigger challenge. While helping a motorist on the side of a road in Massachusetts, he was hit by a car. He lost one leg and the use of the other. But Dubus was not defeated by it. The essays he crafted as he was working through this agony are among the finest I have ever read. They are not maudlin. They use the focus and concentration required to be a great essayist to describe the focus and concentration required to live a life of joy in the midst of pain. His pain put him in even deeper touch with the sacramental realities of everyday life.

> I only have to lie on my bed, waking after Mass has already ended, and I am receiving sacraments with each breath, as I did

while I slept; with each movement of my body as I exercise my lower abdomen to ease the pain in my back caused by sitting for fifteen hours: in my wheelchair, my car, and on my couch, before going to bed for the night; receiving sacraments as I perform crunches and leg lifts, then dress and make the bed while sitting on it. Being at Mass and receiving Communion give me joy and strength. Receiving Communion of desire on my bed does not, for I cannot feel joy with my brain alone. I need sacraments I can receive through my senses. I need God manifested as Christ, who ate and drank and shat and suffered, and laughed. So I can dance with Him as the leaf dances in the breeze under the sun.[1]

My favorite of these essays is easily "Country Road Song." When I teach this essay, I don't lecture. I make the classroom as dark as possible, sit by a small lamp, and read it to them in its entirety. I want them to catch the rhythm of the prose, how it works for Dubus. The writing of the essay was an effort to achieve gratitude by recognizing the grace he had already received, and continues to receive, every day. It's an odd essay that students usually fly through without thinking much about. Dubus describes how he used to run through every season of the year, what he was wearing on each of these runs, what the weather was like, and how his body felt. In the summer he ran in shorts and a bandana, and in the winter he ran with ice in his beard. As the students listen, they perceive that the rhythm of prose is like the rhythm of running and requires the same kind of discipline. Take one step after the other, move forward, push to the end. Runners often say they love having run more than running, and writers say the same about writing. In this case, the achievement is similar: an irreplaceable high. While the runner receives a burst of serotonin, the writer

---

[1]Andre Dubus, *Meditations from a Movable Chair* (New York: Vintage, 1999), 87.

achieves his aim—in this case, a dose of gratitude. Dubus concludes his essay by writing, "I mourn this, and I sing in gratitude for loving this, and in gratitude for all the roads I ran on and walked on, for the hills I climbed and descended, for trees and grass and sky, and for being spared losing running and walking sooner than I did: ten years sooner, or eight seasons, or three; or one day."[2] For the first ten years or so that I taught Dubus, I could not read these lines aloud without tearing up. Depending on what is going on in my life at the moment, these lines can still hit me with full force. None of us are guaranteed even one day of life, much less long life with perfect health. G. K. Chesterton, a student of joy, wrote, "Children are grateful when Santa Claus puts in their stockings gifts of toys or sweets. Could I not be grateful to Santa Claus when he put in my stockings the gift of two miraculous legs?"[3]

Dubus, like Chesterton, teaches us that we receive grace all the time but must achieve gratitude. We achieve gratitude to the exact extent that we recognize how much grace we have already received and continue to receive every single moment of our lives. And that starts with the most miraculous gift of all: the fact that we are here.

THE GIFT OF LIFE

Our age of scientism is trying to convince us that we are biological accidents. If our culture succeeds, it will rob us of gratitude. Gabriel Marcel made the gift of being the cornerstone of his philosophy. "Each one of us is in a position to recognize that his own essence is a gift—that it is not a datum; that he himself is a gift, and that he has no existence at all through himself."[4] Marcel is

---

[2] Dubus, *Meditations*, 108.

[3] G. K. Chesterton, *The Collected Works of G. K. Chesterton, Vol. 1: Heretics, Orthodoxy, the Blatchford Controversies* (San Francisco: Ignatius, 1986), 258.

[4] Gabriel Marcel and Rene Hague, *Mystery of Being, Vol. 2: Faith and Reality* (South Bend, IN: St. Augustine's Press, 2001), 173.

building on an ancient cornerstone of Christian conviction. More than a hundred years earlier, the Catholic bishop François Fénelon wrote, "All is a gift. He who receives the gifts is himself the first gift he receives."[5] And of course St. Augustine, much earlier than that, offers this praise in the first book of his *Confessions*:

> In a living being like me, what shouldn't have amazed, shouldn't have evoked praise? But all those things, such as they are, are gifts from my God. I didn't give them to myself, but they are good gifts, and all of them make up myself. Therefore the one who made me is good, and he himself is my good, and in his name I rejoice in all the good things that comprised me, even as a boy. . . . Thanks be to you, my sweetness and my honor and my faithfulness, my God, thanks be to you for your gifts; but you must preserve them for me, and by doing this you will preserve me, and what you have given me will grow and come to fulfillment, and I will be with you, because it was your gift that I exist at all.[6]

We may know this intellectually, but how can we live and breathe it? How can we invite our students into gratitude just for being alive?

We could begin the way that generations before us have: by remembering the eventuality of death. This is difficult to do in a culture that goes out of its way to forget it. Americans resist grace by preferring to believe in the illusion of control. As one New Yorker put it, "Things may be spinning out of control, but it's, 'I'm eating well, I'm exercising, I'm so damned virtuous, I can do things to my face, I can control my fertility. I'll survive.'"[7] As Albert Borgmann

---

[5]Henri de Lubac, *The Mystery of the Supernatural* (New York: Crossroad, 1998), 77.
[6]Augustine, *Confessions*, trans. Sarah Ruden (New York: Modern Library, 2018), 1.20.31.
[7]Ruth La Ferla, "Outing Death," *The New York Times*, January 20, 2018, www.nytimes .com/2018/01/10/style/death-app-we-croak.html.

explains, the more we believe we have control over our lives, the less able we are to acknowledge that we are recipients of grace.[8]

Ancient cultures know better. There is a Bhutanese folk saying that to be happy one must contemplate death five times a day. Since there must be an app for everything, Hansa Bergwall and Ian Thomas put this wisdom into a $1.99 app called *WeCroak*. If you permit notifications, this app will remind you five times a day, at completely random times, of the fact of your death. The banner simply reads, "Don't forget, you're going to die." If you tap on the banner, you can read a quotation. Because most notifications end up killing my hard-earned productivity trees, *WeCroak* is one of a very few I allow on my phone. Here are some of the quotations I've saved. Eric Sun: "Every day I wake up not-dead is a gift." Hannah Arendt: "Death not merely ends life, it also bestows upon it a silent completeness, snatched from the hazardous flux to which all things human are subject." Ursula LeGuin: "The only thing that makes life possible is permanent, impossible uncertainty: not knowing what comes next." *WeCroak* has a large database of quotations, and the developers add more with each update.

I've used this app for a year now, and I find it bizarrely satisfying. One time I was at my son's bowling tournament when my phone told me I was going to die. This memento mori reminded me that things are not going to be exactly like they are at this moment ever again. I heard the voice of wisdom telling me to look up and enjoy watching him hit that difficult spare. One day I was reading in the hammock, and the notice popped up twice within five minutes. That reminded me that we truly do not know the day or the moment that we will be taken from this life. Now that the

---

[8]"Trouble is often the twin of grace, and if one cannot prosper, neither can the other." Albert Borgmann, *Power Failure: Christianity in the Culture of Technology* (Grand Rapids: Brazos, 2003), 78.

notification flashes on my screen all the time, I've become more desensitized to it. But not entirely. I make a conscious effort to let it sink in. If I find I cannot, I turn off the notification for a week or two to resensitize myself. Sometimes I even reply to it out loud with defiance: "Yes, I am going to die—but not today!" And then I feel newly grateful for my life, health, family, and vocation.

I believe that we became educators because we know—on our better days—that the lives of each one of our students is an irreplaceable gift. We want our students to grasp this truth, to live into their God-given potential. We know that we might end up being the only person who sees that one young student for who he or she is: a unique person, made in the image of God, loved by Jesus, and placed here to give him glory. Is there a more sacred trust?

Of course not. But we cannot keep this trust if we have not learned to see our own lives the same way.

THE GIFT OF TODAY

I have to tell a funny story about the writing of this chapter and the work of gratitude in the so-called dog days of summer. It was July 30, and my husband had given me the joy of a weekend home alone. He took our son to a Cubs-Brewers game in Milwaukee, where he had been asked to serve as visiting priest at a local church. To say I cherish time alone in my own house would be the understatement of the century. I live for this. It was Sunday night, and I was binge-watching a guilty-pleasure television show on our new Apple TV. It was a rare cool evening in the Chicago suburbs, and I had the windows open and the attic fan on. I was very happy. I had planned to go to bed early and get up to write this chapter, thinking to myself, *Last day of July tomorrow—what better time to write the July chapter?* My house was clean, and I had a great bike ride that day and a sous vide New York strip steak for dinner. Perfection.

When our dog, Buddy, licked my elbow that he needed to go out, I snapped on his electric fence collar and opened the back door. He dashed out, yelped, turned tail, and sped right back into the house and plopped onto the sofa. A few seconds later, the odor assaulted me. He had been skunked. We have many skunks where we live in unincorporated Wheaton, and Buddy had been skunked twice before, one time right in the snout by a baby Pepé le Pew. Needless to say, I did not want to adjust my evening plans to wash skunk off of my dog! I texted my husband, grumbling to myself about the timing of this thing, since he would normally be the one to take care of this (with me helping). Instead I had to do it by myself. I didn't want to bother the neighbors. So after more grumbling and a few expletives (I'm human), I took Buddy out back and bathed him three times with OxiClean. This is the best remedy, we've learned the hard way, for a skunking. Hours later I went to bed, trying not to fume as much as the house was. I was moderately successful, perhaps only because I remembered that I was going to try to write about gratitude the next day.

My point in telling this story is to remind us that ordinary life presents constant challenges to a healthy perspective. Perspective is the key to all of this, after all. It is only when I allow an event like a dog skunking to have a bigger place in my thinking than it should that I am robbed of the joy that is ours in Christ. There is, of course, absolutely nothing new in these observations. The challenge is to live it.

How can we keep perspective on the gift of today, skunks and all? We can start with the wisdom of the church calendar. July is smack dab in the middle of what the church calls "ordinary time," a term signifying numbers in a sequence, ordinals ticked off on a calendar. There are two chunks of ordinary time: between Pentecost and Advent (summer into fall), and the shorter period between Christmas and Lent (the most challenging months of winter). Ordinary days, ordinary challenges. Ordinary time is the best place to learn that what you do every day is more important than what you do every once in a while, and that your habits are forming you and impacting the people around you. So ordinary time is the time to build the habit of achieving gratitude into everyday rituals.

One of my favorite passages in Kathleen Norris's *The Quotidian Mysteries* illustrates how. Norris talks about a time when her brother's wife was working as a financial planner in Honolulu, and she would pick up her toddler, Christina, from day care after work. Each day the mother brought her daughter a peeled orange to eat on the ride home. One day Christina was on the porch playing "Mommy's office," and Norris asked her niece what it is she thought her mother did at work. "Without hesitation and with a conviction that I relish to this day, she looked up at me and said, 'She makes oranges.'"

> And that is what God does, I think: makes oranges and wind and the ocean and green leaves and everything else that constitutes our earthly home. Christina's mother had fulfilled a priestly role—priestly in the archetypal sense, in the priesthood of all believers—by allowing the child to participate in a daily ritual, a liturgy of the delicious orange, bright as the sun, sweet with the juice that is the body and blood of this world. The child who is thus fed by a mother's love eventually learns to trust in others and also in God.[9]

The ordinary rituals of our day are saturated with the gift that is creation. When we give to one another, even in the simplicity of

---

[9]Kathleen Norris, *The Quotidian Mysteries: Laundry, Liturgy and "Women's Work"* (New York: Paulist Press, 1998), 67.

a piece of fruit, we are participating in that gift. How much more are we giving in the daily labor of teaching, of setting the fruit on the table day after day after day, inviting the younger generation to the feast? The only work we have to do is to recognize it. O taste and see (Ps 34:8).

When we think of even the most commonplace moments in our classrooms as a kind of liturgy, we help our students to intuit how ordinary time is shot through with the grace of God. Each moment we share together pulsates at the intersection of *kronos* and *kairos*, of measurable time and sacred timelessness. One of the ways that I have attempted to help my students enter that space more deliberately is by adapting the ancient Christian practice of *lectio divina*. Meaning simply "divine reading," *lectio divina* is the practice of slowing down over a handful of sentences of Scripture so that you can hear what God is saying to you through them. At the beginning of the semester I select a portion of a psalm for each class I teach, and then I read aloud that same portion, in the same translation, at least once a week. The procedure is simple: the reader reads slowly over the text one time, waits in silence a full minute, and then reads it, slowly, again. Throughout the semester we will hear that portion at least thirty times together. I also give my students chance to reflect on the fact that we have so little silence in our lives that even one minute of it makes us squirm, which becomes a lesson in itself. If you cannot use Scripture at your school, try a passage or a poem that might serve well as a class mantra. After all, deep listening skills are what our students need now more than ever, and God can speak through anything.

He can even speak through us. It's the greatest privilege we share as educators. And as always, our actions speak what our words can only support or belie. The challenge is clear. For although the young people we welcome into our classrooms are more connected electronically than ever before, they are also more isolated, depressed, and anxious. They are on the verge of a mental health crisis.[10] Satiated by having their every physical need met, their souls are starving. While they have more freedom than any generation before them, the freedom is keeping them in an extended period of adolescence during which they are afraid to launch out and afraid to commit.[11] They need us to model lives lived in gratitude, faithfulness, and love much more than they need to learn math, biology, or history. Let us study this generation so that we can be life-changing educators who love our students from the center of who we are. They are truly starving for it.

FOR ADDITIONAL ENCOURAGEMENT

Calm. Wherever applications are sold.

I know I recommended this application earlier, but I had to put it in again because of what happened today. I was picking up my son from a sleepover, and had my mind set on returning to putting the finishing touches on this book. I got pulled over by a cop for running a stop sign (which I really didn't do). I was angry and thought my workday was shot. I knew I needed to take my own advice — it's just money, and everyone is fine — but couldn't seem to do it. Then I turned to *Calm*, and the daily meditation was on gratitude. There is great power in a well-placed meditation session.

Dubus, Andre. *Meditations from a Movable Chair.* New York: Vintage, 1999.

As I mentioned above, these essays, as well as those in his collection *Broken Vessels*, are a gift to anyone who wants to learn how to receive grace and achieve gratitude. His description of the sacramental beauty of making sandwiches for his girls will make you think about everything we

---

[10]Jean M. Twenge, "Have Smartphones Destroyed a Generation?," *The Atlantic*, September 2017, www.theatlantic.com/magazine/archive/2017/09/has-the-smartphone-destroyed -a-generation/534198/.

[11]Christian Smith and Patricia Snell, *Souls in Transition: The Religious and Spiritual Lives of Emerging Adults* (Oxford: Oxford University Press, 2009), 6.

are able to do without thinking about it in a different light.

Frost, Robert. "The Oven Bird."

> There is a singer everyone has heard,
> Loud, a mid-summer and a mid-wood bird,
> Who makes the solid tree trunks sound again.
> He says that leaves are old and that for flowers
> Mid-summer is to spring as one to ten.
> He says the early petal-fall is past
> When pear and cherry bloom went down in showers
> On sunny days a moment overcast;
> And comes that other fall we name the fall.
> He says the highway dust is over all.
> The bird would cease and be as other birds
> But that he knows in singing not to sing.
> The question that he frames in all but words
> Is what to make of a diminished thing.

Like all good poetry, this poem articulates something that I wouldn't be able to without it. I call it "the oven-bird problem": the feeling you get in the middle of summer that summer is going to end and spring is far away, and it ruins your joy. If you know how to solve the oven-bird problem, will you write and tell me?

Five-Minute Journal. Intelligent Change.

This is one of many resources that guide you to spend a little time each morning and evening to reflect on what you are grateful for. If you prefer electronic versions, there are many apps, including some that allow you to insert photographs.

Smith, Christian, and Patricia Snell. *Souls in Transition: The Religious and Spiritual Lives of Emerging Adults.* Oxford: Oxford University Press, 2009.

Wheaton faculty had the opportunity to hear Christian Smith reflect on his research, and it was very helpful. We need to be students of our students. This book will help you to understand where they are in their spiritual lives and how the broader culture is impacting their choices.

WeCroak. Wherever applications are sold.

"Don't forget, you're going to die." It's going to happen someday. Enjoy the present moment.

Epilogue

Leap Year

As everyone who has ever written a book knows, the process takes a lot of time. When I got this manuscript back from the editor, he very kindly and gently suggested that I add a conclusion, because otherwise I would be ending my book with a blatant reminder that we are all going to die one day.

Of course he was right. But getting to the end of the final revision process and having to write a conclusion was not something I wanted to do. It reminded me of the time that the editor of my first book (on Flannery O'Connor) asked for a conclusion that I had to produce practically overnight. In the year between submitting what I thought was the final manuscript and receiving this editorial direction, I had moved on to other projects. I simply wasn't in the headspace of that book any more. So I was annoyed and frustrated, and did not want to do it. When I was sharing my woes with my colleague and friend David Wright, he suggested that I use the opportunity to show how my research into O'Connor's work led me to the project I was working on at the time. It was brilliant advice. It helped me to enjoy writing the conclusion because I got to clarify what to others may not have been so clear: my scholarly trajectory.

Taking a lesson from that experience, I decided to enjoy this opportunity to more fully ponder and share what happened to me in the intervening year between completing this manuscript and receiving the edited version. I submitted the manuscript during the fall term, just before what ended up being the most difficult spring semester in my career as an educator. I cannot go into specifics, but I had two situations in which the content of my teaching was challenged. In one situation, a student's parent called the president of the college to complain about what I was teaching. To make matters worse—and with some kind of cosmic irony— both of these events happened in February and March, which as you now know are my most challenging months. In between the two situations, another crown cracked and led to the loss of that tooth. A whole month's pay, right into my mouth. As is the case with many stressful situations, I didn't recognize at the time how much the experience of having to defend myself and to fall on my sword drained me. I was not flourishing, but withering on the vine. In retrospect I'm not surprised that when the summer finally arrived, instead of going right into my scholarly work as I usually do, I hit the skids. Reader, I completely burned out. I knew better than to try to accomplish anything that May, but when June came and went, I still didn't have it. I began to panic.

As always, my friends saved me from despair. They reminded me that the events of that spring did more damage to me than I might have recognized, and that it would be more than fine for me to take the summer completely off—a Jubilee summer. I would probably have done this anyway, but it was far superior and much more nourishing to do it with grace toward myself rather than rancor and judgment. So I let the summer renew me. I took a long, silent retreat at a facility in Michigan called the Hermitage. (They have a cabin named "Thoreau" that borders a pond—what's not to love?) I watched a lot of HGTV and made detailed plans to update our house in ways it had needed for a long time. I Marie Kondo-ed my clothes. I turned the master bath into a Scandinavian spa. I read a lot of books in the hammock. I took two family vacations and did not try to do any work on them. It was a good summer, and I was certainly more ready for the fall semester than I would have been if I had tried to push through the burnout.

As my energy for teaching began only very slowly to return, it occurred to me that all this happened just before the year prior to my next possible sabbatical. It makes perfect sense. The break felt too far off to look forward to, and I felt trapped. A friend recommended the book *Burnout*, by Emily and Amelia Nagoski. The writers explain how women who are in the giving professions — like teaching — are particularly prone to burning out. Even when we are the primary breadwinners of the family, we usually end up being responsible for most of the domestic work, especially when our children are small. In short, we are already giving away precious energy to serving others, and then we go off to work to face more of the same. The authors explain that it is not usually large stressors, but the accumulation of "chronic, mild stress" that get us in the end. "In the twenty-first century West, 'one damn thing after another' is what being a woman often feels like. It's a constant, low-level stream of stressors that are out of your control. Most individual examples are little more than an annoyance . . . but they accumulate."[1]

Whether you are a man or a woman, single or married, younger or older, teaching is a giving profession and it is hard to flourish when one's roots have grown dry. What I learned from reading this book — a little too late to help with the guilt — was that what I did

---

[1] Emily Nagoski and Amelia Nagoski, *Burnout: The Secret to Unlocking the Stress Cycle* (New York: Ballantine Books, 2019), 84.

that summer was the best thing I could have done. I used a different part of my brain to organize, paint, and wallpaper my house. Accomplishing *anything*, the authors of *Burnout* point out, helps to knock us out of the feeling of being helpless. I'm so glad I listened to my friends and let myself have that Jubilee summer. Maybe it's time for yours too.

We all became teachers because we want to give ourselves away. We care more about giving young people what they need to flourish than we care about recognition, accolades, or financial rewards. But that doesn't mean that we don't grow weary of the fact that often the most valuable parts of what we do are invisible to others, even to the students themselves. The office hours where we end up playing the part of therapist. The night spent preparing to teach a text we know can be life changing. The fifteen letters of recommendation we are responsible for—due right before Christmas. The extra time spent helping that one student struggling with her writing, even though all she seems to care about is the grade. It is above all important to remember that God sees all of these efforts. "And whenever you pray, do not be like the hypocrites; for they love to stand and pray in the synagogues and at the street corners, so that they may be seen by others. Truly I tell you, they have received their reward. But whenever you pray, go into your room and shut the door and pray to your Father who is in secret; and your Father who sees in secret will reward you" (Mt 6:5-6). What is teaching if it is not a sincere prayer that our students flourish?

It may be an overused quotation now, but it is no less true for that. Frederick Buechner, writing about vocation, reminds us that "neither the hair shirt nor the soft berth will do" when we are trying to figure out how to spend the precious time that we have been given. Instead, "the place God calls you to is the place

where your deep gladness and the world's deep hunger meet."[2]
There is no deeper gladness than teaching, and no deeper hunger
than that of our young people. They hunger for the peace that
passes understanding and the love that gives us the ability to
love others. As we pray yet again for the ability to "embrace the
lace" and flourish in the coming academic year, let's thank God
that we can claim with confidence that being an educator is the
greatest profession in the world. Let us go forth to love and serve
the Lord by living out our calling with gladness and singleness
of heart. With joy.

Amen.

---

[2]Frederick Buechner, *Wishful Thinking: A Seeker's ABC*, rev. and exp. ed. (San Francisco: HarperOne, 1993), 119.

Bibliography

Allen, David, and James Fallows. *Getting Things Done: The Art of Stress-Free Productivity*. Revised edition. New York: Penguin Books, 2015.

Atwell, Nancie. *In the Middle: A Lifetime of Learning About Writing, Reading, and Adolescents*. Third edition. Portsmouth, NH: Heinemann, 2014.

Augustine. *Confessions*. Translated by Sarah Ruden. New York: Modern Library, 2018.

Bain, Ken. *What the Best College Teachers Do*. Cambridge, MA: Harvard University Press, 2004.

Bass, Dorothy, and Craig Dykstra. *Teaching and Christian Practices: Reshaping Faith and Learning*. Edited by David I. Smith and James K. A. Smith. Grand Rapids, MI: Eerdmans, 2011.

Baumeister, Roy F., and John Tierney. *Willpower: Rediscovering the Greatest Human Strength*. New York: Penguin Books, 2012.

Bonhoeffer, Dietrich. *Life Together: The Classic Exploration of Faith in Community*. San Francisco: HarperOne, 2009.

Borgmann, Albert. *Power Failure: Christianity in the Culture of Technology*. Grand Rapids, MI: Brazos Press, 2003.

Brown, Brené. *Daring Greatly: How the Courage to Be Vulnerable Transforms the Way We Live, Love, Parent, and Lead*. Reprint edition. New York: Avery, 2015.

Burge, Gary M. *Mapping Your Academic Career: Charting the Course of a Professor's Life*. Downers Grove, IL: IVP Academic, 2015.

Cairns, Scott. *The End of Suffering: Finding Purpose in Pain*. Brewster, MA: Paraclete Press, 2009.

Carlson, Richard, and Joseph Bailey. *Slowing Down to the Speed of Life: How to Create a More Peaceful, Simpler Life from the Inside Out*. San Francisco: HarperOne, 2009.

Carnes, Mark C. *Minds on Fire: How Role-Immersion Games Transform College*. Reprint edition. Cambridge, MA: Harvard University Press, 2018.

Chesterton, G. K. *Heretics, Orthodoxy, the Blatchford Controversies*. Edited by David Dooley. Vol. 1 of *The Collected Works of G. K. Chesterton*. San Francisco: Ignatius Press, 1986.

Clarkson, Sally, and Nathan Clarkson. *Different: The Story of an Outside-the-Box Kid and the Mom Who Loved Him*. Carol Stream, IL: Tyndale House Publishers, 2017.

Conn, Peter. "The Great Accreditation Farce." *The Chronicle of Higher Education*, June 30, 2014. www.chronicle.com/article/The-Great-Accreditation-Farce/147425.

Crosby, Cindy. *Waiting for Morning: Hearing God's Voice in the Darkness*. Grand Rapids, MI: Baker, 2001.

Csikszentmihalyi, Mihaly. *Finding Flow: The Psychology of Engagement with Everyday Life*. New York: Basic Books, 1998.

Csikszentmihalyi, Mihaly. *Flow: The Psychology of Optimal Experience*. New York: Harper Perennial Modern Classics, 2008.

Davidson, Cathy N., and Danica Savonick. "Gender Bias in Academe: An Annotated Bibliography of Important Recent Studies." *HASTAC*, January 26, 2015. www.hastac.org/blogs/superadmin/2015/01/26/gender-bias-academe-annotated-bibliography-important-recent-studies.

Dawn, Marva J. *Keeping the Sabbath Wholly: Ceasing, Resting, Embracing, Feasting*. Grand Rapids, MI: Eerdmans, 1989.

Delbanco, Andrew. *College: What It Was, Is, and Should Be*. Princeton, NJ: Princeton University Press, 2014.

Dillard, Annie. *Pilgrim at Tinker Creek*. New York: Harper Perennial Modern Classics, 2013.

Dubus, Andre. *Meditations from a Movable Chair*. New York: Vintage, 1999.

Duhigg, Charles. *The Power of Habit: Why We Do What We Do in Life and Business*. New York: Random House, 2014.

Epstein, Mikhail, and Igor Klyukanov. *The Transformative Humanities: A Manifesto*. London: Bloomsbury, 2012.

Foster, Richard J. *Celebration of Discipline: The Path to Spiritual Growth*. Special anniversary edition. New York: HarperOne, 2018.

Frost, Robert. *Complete Poems of Robert Frost*. New York: Holt, Rinehart and Winston, 1949.

Hagerty, Barbara Bradley. *Life Reimagined: The Science, Art, and Opportunity of Midlife*. Reprint edition. New York: Riverhead Books, 2017.

Hanh, Thich Nhat. *Your True Home: The Everyday Wisdom of Thich Nhat Hanh: 365 Days of Practical, Powerful Teachings from the Beloved Zen Teacher*. Edited by Melvin McLeod. Boston: Shambhala, 2011.

Hanh, Thich Nhat, and H. H. the Dalai Lama. *Peace Is Every Step: The Path of Mindfulness in Everyday Life*. Edited by Arnold Kotler. New York: Bantam, 1992.

Hart, David Bentley. *The Experience of God: Being, Consciousness, Bliss*. New Haven, CT: Yale University Press, 2014.

Heschel, Abraham Joshua, and Susannah Heschel. *The Sabbath*. New York: Farrar, Straus and Giroux, 2005.

Huffington, Arianna. *Thrive: The Third Metric to Redefining Success and Creating a Life of Well-Being, Wisdom, and Wonder*. Reprint edition. New York: Harmony Books, 2015.

Julian of Norwich, and Father John-Julian, OJN. *The Complete Julian of Norwich*. Brewster, MA: Paraclete Press, 2009.

Keller, Gary, and Jay Papasan. *The ONE Thing: The Surprisingly Simple Truth Behind Extraordinary Results*. Austin, TX: Bard Press, 2013.

Kondo, Marie. *The Life-Changing Magic of Tidying Up: The Japanese Art of Decluttering and Organizing*. Berkeley, CA: Ten Speed Press, 2014.

La Ferla, Ruth. "Outing Death." *New York Times*, Jan. 20, 2018. www.nytimes .com/2018/01/10/style/death-app-we-croak.html.

Laird, Martin. *Into the Silent Land: A Guide to the Christian Practice of Contemplation*. Oxford: Oxford University Press, 2006.

Lamott, Anne. *Bird by Bird: Some Instructions on Writing and Life*. New York: Anchor, 1995.

Lang, James M. "How to Prepare for Class Without Overpreparing." *The Chronicle of Higher Education*, July 2018. www.chronicle.com/article/How -to-Prepare-for-Class/244015.

Lang, James M. *Small Teaching: Everyday Lessons from the Science of Learning*. San Francisco, CA: Jossey-Bass, 2016.

Leiva-Merikakis, Erasmo. *Fire of Mercy, Heart of the Word: Meditations on the Gospel According to Saint Matthew*. San Francisco, CA: Ignatius Press, 1996.

Levertov, Denise. *The Stream & the Sapphire: Selected Poems on Religious Themes*. New York: New Directions, 1997.

Lewis, C. S. *Till We Have Faces: A Myth Retold*. Reissue edition. New York: HarperOne, 2017.

Lubac, Henri de. *The Mystery of the Supernatural*. New York: Crossroad, 1998.

Mazzarella, Nicole. *This Heavy Silence: A Novel*. Brewster, MA: Paraclete Press, 2006.

McGonigal, Kelly. *The Willpower Instinct: How Self-Control Works, Why It Matters, and What You Can Do to Get More of It*. Reprint edition. New York: Avery, 2013.

McRaven, William H. *Make Your Bed: Little Things That Can Change Your Life . . . and Maybe the World*. 2nd edition. New York: Grand Central Publishing, 2017.

Morrison, Toni. *Beloved*. Reprint edition. New York: Vintage, 2004.

Nagoski, Emily, and Amelia Nagoski. *Burnout: The Secret to Unlocking the Stress Cycle*. New York: Ballantine Books, 2019.

Neuhaus, Richard John. *Death on a Friday Afternoon: Meditations on the Last Words of Jesus from the Cross*. New York: Basic Books, 2001.

Newport, Cal. *Deep Work: Rules for Focused Success in a Distracted World*. New York: Grand Central Publishing, 2018.

Nietzsche, Friedrich. *The Essential Nietzsche: Beyond Good and Evil and the Genealogy of Morals*. New York: Chartwell Books, 2017.

Norris, Kathleen. *Acedia & Me: A Marriage, Monks, and a Writer's Life*. Reprint edition. New York: Riverhead Books, 2010.

Norris, Kathleen. *The Cloister Walk*. New York: Riverhead Books, 1997.

Norris, Kathleen. *The Quotidian Mysteries: Laundry, Liturgy and "Women's Work."* New York: Paulist Press, 1998.

Nouwen, Henri J. M. *The Return of the Prodigal Son: A Story of Homecoming*. Reissue edition. New York: Image Books, 1994.

O'Connor, Flannery. *Collected Works*. New York: Library of America, 1988.

Palmer, Parker J. *The Courage to Teach: Exploring the Inner Landscape of a Teacher's Life*. 10th anniversary edition. San Francisco, CA: Jossey-Bass, 2007.

Palmer, Parker J. *To Know as We Are Known: Education as a Spiritual Journey*. Reprint edition. San Francisco, CA: HarperOne, 1993.

Pieper, Josef, and James V. Schall. *Leisure: The Basis of Culture*. San Francisco, CA: Ignatius Press, 2009.

Rauch, Jonathan. "What Teenage Turmoil and Midlife Crises Have in Common." *Atlantic*, April 22, 2018. https://www.theatlantic.com/magazine/archive/2018/05/jonathan-rauch-adolescence/556865/.

Robinson, Marilynne. *Gilead*. New York: Farrar, Straus and Giroux, 2004.

Rohr, Richard. *Falling Upward: A Spirituality for the Two Halves of Life*. San Francisco, CA: Jossey-Bass, 2011.

Romm, Cari. "Where Age Equals Happiness." *Atlantic*, November 6, 2014. https://www.theatlantic.com/health/archive/2014/11/where-age-equals-happiness/382434/.

Rubin, Gretchen. *Better Than Before: What I Learned About Making and Breaking Habits—to Sleep More, Quit Sugar, Procrastinate Less, and Generally Build a Happier Life*. New York: Broadway Books, 2015.

Rubin, Gretchen. *The Four Tendencies: The Indispensable Personality Profiles That Reveal How to Make Your Life Better*. New York: Harmony, 2017.

Rubin, Gretchen. *The Happiness Project: Or, Why I Spent a Year Trying to Sing in the Morning, Clean My Closets, Fight Right, Read Aristotle, and Generally Have More Fun.* Revised edition. New York: Harper Paperbacks, 2015.

Russell, Helen. *The Year of Living Danishly: Uncovering the Secrets of the World's Happiest Country.* Reissue edition. London: Icon Books, 2016.

Sertillanges, A. G., OP, and James V. Schall, SJ. *The Intellectual Life: Its Spirit, Conditions, Methods.* Translated by Mary Ryan. Reprint edition. Washington, DC: Catholic University of America Press, 1992.

Shipman, Matt. "Online Students Give Instructors Higher Marks If They Think Instructors Are Men." *NC State News*, December 9, 2014. https://news.ncsu.edu /2014/12/macnell-gender-2014/.

Silvia, Paul J. *How to Write a Lot: A Practical Guide to Productive Academic Writing.* Washington, DC: American Psychological Association, 2007.

Slaughter, Anne-Marie. *Unfinished Business: Women Men Work Family.* New York: Random House, 2016.

Slaughter, Anne-Marie. "Why Women Still Can't Have It All." *Atlantic*, June 13, 2012, www.theatlantic.com/magazine/archive/2012/07/why-women-still-cant -have-it-all/309020/.

Smith, Christian, and Patricia Snell. *Souls in Transition: The Religious and Spiritual Lives of Emerging Adults.* Oxford: Oxford University Press, 2009.

Smith, James K. A. *You Are What You Love: The Spiritual Power of Habit.* Grand Rapids, MI: Brazos Press, 2016.

Stevenson, Robert Louis. *The Strange Case of Dr. Jekyll and Mr. Hyde.* Mineola, NY: Dover Publications, 1991.

Thoreau, Henry David. *Natural History Essays.* Revised edition. Layton, UT: Gibbs Smith, 2011.

Thoreau, Henry David, et al. *The Writings of Henry David Thoreau: Excursions, and Poems.* Palala Press, 2018.

Thoreau, Henry David. *Walden: A Fully Annotated Edition.* Edited by Jeffrey S. Cramer. Annotated edition. New Haven, CT: Yale University Press, 2004.

Twenge, Jean M. "Have Smartphones Destroyed a Generation?" *Atlantic*, September 2017. www.theatlantic.com/magazine/archive/2017/09/has-the-smart phone-destroyed-a-generation/534198/.

Undset, Sigrid, and Brad Leithauser. *Kristin Lavransdatter.* Edited by Tiina Nunnally. New York: Penguin Classics, 2005.

Vaillant, George E. *Aging Well: Surprising Guideposts to a Happier Life from the Landmark Harvard Study of Adult Development.* Reprint edition. Boston: Little, Brown and Company, 2003.

Warren, Tish Harrison. *Liturgy of the Ordinary: Sacred Practices in Everyday Life*. Downers Grove, IL: InterVarsity Press, 2016.

Wiking, Meik. *The Little Book of Hygge: Danish Secrets to Happy Living*. New York: William Morrow, 2017.

Williams, William Carlos. *The Collected Poems of William Carlos Williams*. New York: New Directions Publishing, 1991.

Wiman, Christian, ed. *Joy: 100 Poems*. New Haven, CT: Yale University Press, 2017.

Finding the Textbook You Need

The IVP Academic Textbook Selector
is an online tool for instantly finding the IVP books
suitable for over 250 courses across 24 disciplines.

ivpacademic.com